W9-AXD-187

CHANGE
IS YOUR
COMPETITIVE
ADVANTAGE

CHANGE
IS YOUR
COMPETITIVE
ADVANTAGE

STRATEGIES FOR ADAPTING, TRANSFORMING, AND SUCCEEDING IN THE NEW BUSINESS REALITY

Karl G. Schoemer, MS
founder of VisionQuest

BUSINESS

Avon, Massachusetts

Published by Adams Business, an imprint of
Adams Media, a division of F+W Media, Inc.
57 Littlefield Street, Avon, MA 02322. U.S.A.
www.adamsmedia.com

ISBN 10: 1-59869-801-X
ISBN 13: 978-1-59869-801-5

Printed in the United States of America.

J I H G F E D

Library of Congress Cataloging-in-Publication Data
is available from the publisher.

This publication is designed to provide accurate and authoritative information with regard to the subject matter covered. It is sold with the understanding that the publisher is not engaged in rendering legal, accounting, or other professional advice. If legal advice or other expert assistance is required, the services of a competent professional person should be sought.
　　—From a *Declaration of Principles* jointly adopted by a Committee of the American Bar Association and a Committee of Publishers and Associations

Many of the designations used by manufacturers and sellers to distinguish their product are claimed as trademarks. Where those designations appear in this book and Adams Media was aware of a trademark claim, the designations have been printed with initial capital letters.

This book is available at quantity discounts for bulk purchases.
For information, please call 1-800-289-0963.

CONTENTS

ACKNOWLEDGMENTS

A decade or more ago, I had a decision to make. Should I return to school at an advanced age to pursue my Doctorate Degree, or should I immerse myself in my business and my clients? Given the lack of letters after my name, it is clear I chose the latter—and I have never looked back. I can honestly say that the last ten or fifteen years have been the best education I could ever hope for. Everything I know has been taught to me or refined and improved by my clients. I believe the opportunity to work closely with, listen to, learn from, and absorb and process the real life challenges that my clients deal with has made me a far better author, speaker, consultant, and trainer. I once heard it proposed that we are composed of little bits of all the people we have encountered in our lives. I believe that. Therefore, I also believe that my knowledge, approach to change, and beliefs are the sum of all those I have had the privilege of working for, and working with. So to all my clients, over all these years, Thank You!

Thank you to my family for I am the sum of their influence, love, and support. Ann, thank you for your unwavering support and for so expertly managing our lives while I was away at "school." Thank you Erin, Kate, and Frank for who you are, who you make me, and for teaching me about life everyday. Thank you Kenny for all that you do for me, and all that you have taught me. Thank you Dave for being a best friend and one of the smartest people I know.

An extra special thank you goes to Marissa. You have been a friend, a colleague, an inspiration, and a blessing in my life. This book and many, many other projects and efforts would still be sitting on the credenza without your support, prodding, contribution, and belief.

Thank you to everyone at Adams Media who believes in me and my messages enough to publish this book. A special thanks to Gary, Amy, and Stacie, as well as a big thank you to Ed Walters and thanks to Wendy, Colleen, and Peter.

And most importantly . . . thanks to you . . . the reader. I hope these insights benefit you in ways that you don't even anticipate today.

INTRODUCTION

Over the last fifteen years, I've had the opportunity to travel around the world and work with hundreds of companies and organizations, and thousands of individuals, as they were undergoing change. During that time, I've seen some things that people and organizations do well during times of change. Mostly, though, I've seen all the headaches that people and organizations encounter when trying to cope with something new.

The main difference (all right, *change*) I've noticed since I started helping people deal with these issues is this: Fifteen—or even five—years ago, I would work with people and organizations during what was considered a "time of change." A company was revising its management structure, or its way of doing business, and its employees had to learn how to deal with the changes that entailed. We'd hold some meetings to clear the air and to impart some strategies for coping with the change, and then it was, "All right, everybody, let's get back to work."

As the pace of business and society has accelerated, and as waves of change have crashed one atop another, it is no longer possible to think of change as something to be dealt with, gotten through, and then no longer worried about until the next change happens. What was once considered a "period of change" is now known as

"Thursday." *Every* day in your company or organization is one where you have to work hard to manage change, deal with its aftershocks, and anticipate the newest development racing around the corner and heading straight at you. There's no longer something called "work" to get back to. The "work" today includes dealing with daily change.

But even in this new era of perpetual change, a few things that have always been true about change remain so. Here's the first one:

Nobody likes change.

The people in your organization resist change, and you do too—we all do. This is only natural. After all, the goal of each person working in a company or organization is (or at least used to be) to become really, really good at what he or she does. After mastering a job, no one wants to then be told: "What you're doing is really great. Now just do it differently ... faster ... for another market ... under different management ... in a new location ... with the software we just switched to ... using this new process...." And so on. Considering how difficult and uncomfortable change is, some resistance (and grumbling and complaining) is inevitable. My goal in this book is not to tell you how to eliminate all resistance to change in your organization. You can change many things, but human nature is not one of them. What you'll learn here is *why* and *how* people (including yourself) resist change and what strategies you can use to lessen that resistance and help people get through the phases of a change as quickly and easily as possible.

Here's another thing about changes within businesses and organizations that was true in the past and still is:

When you change how you do things, your productivity always goes down.

This may seem counterintuitive. After all, isn't the whole *point* of making a change to increase your productivity . . . your efficiency . . . your profits? Why are you even making a change if it will make things worse?

The explanation for this is that the above sentence is not quite complete. What I really mean to say is:

When you change how you do things, your productivity always goes down *initially*.

Sometimes you will in fact make a change that really would harm your productivity permanently. That means that you've made a bad decision, and you'll have to make another change to correct course. But even if you make the best change available, and do everything possible to help the people in your organization adapt to it quickly (as you'll learn to in this book!), your productivity will *still* go down at first. Every major change brings with it some resistance, problems, adjustments, and more. Put together, these will put a drag on your productivity, just as surely as the forces of air resistance and gravity will inevitably drag a golf ball you hit back to the ground.

I'm not going to promise to show you how to completely eliminate the initial drop in productivity caused by change—anymore than I can point out loopholes in the laws of physics that will help your golf game. The drop is *gonna* happen. The key, as we'll discuss in this book, is to make the hit to your organization's operation as small and as short-lived as possible. You need to manage the *depth* and *duration* (two words you'll also see later) of the damage to your productivity and move as quickly as possible to the stage where a change pays off as intended.

In *Change Is Your Competitive Advantage* you're going to discover how the ever-faster pace of change has a make-or-break impact on businesses and organizations today. I'll show you how to get you and your colleagues through the stages of change as quickly and smoothly as possible, with as small a downturn in your operation as you can manage. And if I were writing this book even five years ago, I could wrap things up there. But one result of what I call "the New Business Reality" (a concept I'll explain in Chapter 2) is that merely coping with and managing change is no longer enough.

The truth is, as someone working for a business or organization today, you already manage change. I think you manage change every day, simply because you have no choice. Now, after you learn the strategies in this book, I really believe you will get much better at understanding and managing change. But I also believe that we are at the point in business today where simply managing change is not enough to be successful. We actually have to *seize* change and make it a part of our competitive advantage. We have to be able to take advantage of all of the opportunities that come our way every day because of all of this change. So here is a fact about change and business that was *not* true a few years ago, but is crucially so today:

Your career success depends not on doing well what you've done in the past but on changing quickly and effectively so that you can do what needs to be done in the future.

To put it another way, your greatest value to your organization is not the set of specific, learned skills you bring to your job. Your real value lies in the ability you have to be a change agent. To be successful in the New Business Reality, you need to be able to master change, help others adapt to change, and use this ability to gain a competitive advantage for yourself within your organization and for your business or organization within its marketplace. Boosting your career and your company's success through seizing that edge is what this book is all about. (Note: Throughout the book, you'll find "Managing Up" sidebars, geared toward individuals, and "Managing Down" sidebars, geared toward leaders.)

managing UP

CAREER SECURITY

When asked how the way she evaluated job candidates had changed over the past few years, Anne Mulcahy, chairwoman and chief executive of the Xerox Corporation, told Adam Bryant of *The New York Times* that she looked more for "adaptability and flexibility. One of the things that is mind-boggling right now is how much we have to change all the time."

How will we get there? Well, in these pages I'll explain how the New Business Reality is a time of increasingly faster change, greater insecurity, but also great opportunity. We'll see how change, and the resistance and loss of productivity that goes along with it, is the biggest challenge facing businesses today. Then we will explore how you and the people in your organization react to change, and the communication you need to encourage in order to get through it. We'll also look at a number of different techniques for dealing with change. The most crucial part of the book discusses how to remake your organization so that it's always ready for change, and how to seize a competitive advantage for your business today and tomorrow.

Along the way, I'll give you the information and tools you need in a variety of ways. Those will include:

Explanations of the dynamics of change, drawn from my years of experience working with organizations in the middle of it

Some on-point examples from business, technology, and society that provide lessons about the challenges of change

Stories of a company dealing with many different aspects of change

Sets of "tools you can use" that give you specific strategies for mastering change

We're going to talk about "change" in a lot of contexts here: changes in the marketplace, changes in your own workplace, and changes in how you and your organization do things. But the most important type of change—by far—I'm concerned with is this one: *a change in your way of thinking and behaving.* What I'm aiming for in this book is to challenge your thinking, interrupt your everyday patterns, and try to get you to see things from a different point of view. You may not agree with or be able to put into practice everything you'll find here. (In fact, I'm assuming you won't.) What I will ask, though, is that you think seriously about what we discuss and how it relates to your own career. Surrounded by ever-faster change, it can be nearly impossible to take a moment to look at the big picture. We're too focused on just getting by and on finishing things that really should have been done yesterday—or in the New Business Reality, abandoned last week.

My hope is that after reading *Change Is Your Competitive Advantage* you'll find that while change is unending, unsettling, and often uncomfortable, it also offers tremendous opportunities to those who know how to master it. Once you change your thinking, and change your behavior, something else becomes possible—a very positive change in the success of your career and your organization.

CHANGE IS YOUR COMPETITIVE ADVANTAGE

01

CHANGE—FAST TODAY, AND EVEN FASTER TOMORROW

Think about it for a minute: What are some changes that you've experienced in your business or organization over the last year or two?

In fact, don't just think about it: Get out a sheet of paper and a pen. (You may want to get a few sheets, actually, as you'll need some for later in the book.) Consider what working at your business was like two years ago (or whenever you started working there), including such aspects as your work itself, your colleagues, your company, your market, and so on. Then jot down five or six things that are different about it now.

If your business is like the ones I've done workshops with, you might come up with things like:

- Increased pace of work
- Different management structure
- Changes in the marketplace
- New policies from the human resources department
- Different office
- New systems and software
- Higher expectations
- Different colleagues and bosses

- Changes in mood and morale (and usually not for the better)
- Different procedures
- New competitors
- . . . and possibly more.

That's an awful lot to cope with in a relatively short period of time. One result of having to deal with all this change is that it creates a business environment very different from the one of five or ten years ago and just about unrecognizable from what people faced twenty or thirty years back.

In this part of the book, we'll look into how the dynamics of change affect your business and how the ever-accelerating pace of change has led to the New Business Reality—a reality that is full of challenges and insecurity, but also excitement and opportunities.

WHERE CHANGE COMES FROM

Now ask yourself one big question about the changes that have occurred in your own organization: *Why?* What is driving all the changes—in pace, expectations, requirements, technology, leadership, and more—that you're experiencing? Where are they coming from?

I've worked with a lot of organizations filled with a lot of people who walk around saying things like: "You know, things used to be great around here. But now my boss is forcing me to change too fast or too much. Why can't he leave well enough alone? If my boss would just get off my back and let me do my job like I know how, everything would be okay."

I'm sorry to have to break it to anyone who is thinking that way—I know how fun it is to blame everything on the higher-ups—but the problem is really not your boss. It is not your boss's boss. It is not the CEO of the corporation or a new VP trying to make her mark in the company. The truth is, it's the *entire world around you* that is forcing your organization to change. You don't have to look far to realize you are not the only organization, industry, and profession undergoing change. Just pick up the newspaper or watch the business news any morning. You'll see a lot of organizations undergoing a lot of changes for a lot of different reasons.

I call all of this the "winds of change." These winds of change are not only blowing in corporate America but around the world as well. And because of the greater interconnectivity of people, businesses, and societies across the globe—what Thomas Friedman is referring to in his best-selling book about how "the world is flat"— the reality is that change everywhere else ends up causing change where you are. The true source of change in your organization is not internal but external. To blame your boss for the inevitable effects of the winds of change is like blaming the weatherman for telling you there will be a blizzard tomorrow. Whether the weatherman tells you about it or not, you're still going to have a foot of snow to shovel in the morning.

WHAT DRIVES CHANGE? HERE'S A TIP

Let me give you a TIP. There are three basic factors that drive change. And, as you might have guessed by those capital letters, they begin with the letters *T, I,* and *P.*

Let's start with the first one: *Technology.*

You know this already. Technology is a driver of change. Most of the visible changes in your workplace today, as compared to twenty or thirty years ago, are a result of the different technologies we use to communicate with each other, manage our businesses, and create our products or services. And the one engine that drives technological change more than any other is the advance in computing capabilities.

In 1965 Gordon Moore, a microchip pioneer and one of the founders of Intel, made a prediction that helps to explain not only why computer technology has improved, but also why this improvement has moved faster and faster to enable the accelerating the pace of change we see today. Moore observed the rate at which the capacity of newer microchips was increasing, and he came up with what became known as Moore's Law. It states: *The capacity of computing power contained on a single microchip will double every two years.* (In another version of this law, Moore believed the doubling might even occur every eighteen months.) Moore's Law later came with a corollary: *As computing power doubles, its cost will decrease to half as much.* In other words, every two years will bring twice the computing power at half the price.

What can Moore's Law and its corollary tell us? Well, for one thing, they explain why it is that every time you buy a computer, you see an ad three months—or three days—later for a similar one that has more power and costs three hundred dollars less. More generally, they help to explain how technology manages to change at an ever-growing pace, as advances feed upon themselves. Not every change in our lives is driven by technology, and not every technological change is driven by computers (though most are, at least indirectly). But the exponential growth in computing power is a big part in the faster change we see today.

THE POWER OF DOUBLING

To understand the explosive growth that comes with doubling something every two years, you only need to take a quick look at the numbers. Things that grow at a relatively stable 3 to 8 percent a year—prices, let's say—will become two to four times as large over a twenty-year period. Look at old ads or car prices and you can see that's true. When something doubles every two years, though, twenty years later its growth will reach 2 to the tenth power, or 1,024. In other words, Moore's Law holds that computer capacity can become about *one thousand* times as great over that period.

And over the following twenty years, it can reach one thousand times as high as that new point, or *one million* times greater than where it started. Overall technological change increases at nowhere near that rate, of course, but the high growth rate of technological development does trickle down to affect change everywhere.

A LOT OF KNOWLEDGE CAN BE A DANGEROUS THING

The second letter in TIP brings us to the second force behind change: *Information.*

It's been said that there has been more information produced in the last thirty years than mankind produced in the previous five thousand. One weekday edition of the *New York Times* may have more information in it than the average person would have access to in his lifetime in eighteenth-century England.

They say the information available to us doubles every five years. As everything else increases in speed, I think that this is an old fact. By now, the information available to us may be doubling faster—perhaps every two years, even. And we know how quickly doubling something every two years can lead to an enormous change.

Information and Organizations

The increase in the amount of information that exists—and particularly in the amount that is easily *available* to you—has huge implications for your business or organization. You have access to much more information on your market than businesses did in the past. You can find more books, articles, blogs, cable-television shows (and on and on) to give you information that may help in making business decisions. When looking for new employees, you don't have to consider only those who happen to see a help-wanted ad in your local paper. You can reach out on the Internet through a variety of means to find potential employees; and, when you are considering hiring one, you can do web searches to verify her background.

This greater information works both ways. Customers no longer have to rely on the local yellow pages to find businesses to deal with. And, with all the information they can glean from sources like the expanding media, Internet message boards, and websites like ePinions.com, customers know a lot more about the products they buy and the businesses they deal with than in the past. As for the people you're trying to hire, they too can find out more about your organization—and other potential employers—before deciding to work for you.

managing *DOWN*

THE PRICE OF NEW TECHNOLOGY

Don't require your staff to use any technology you can't or wouldn't use yourself. It may seem like a lot of trouble to learn new systems—but your employees are watching to see whether you're really committed to the new tools.

The ever-increasing information in the world today requires a change in how you think of your business; just to keep up, you have to consider the marketplace more broadly and learn about it more deeply. It also requires a change in how you operate your organization. You need to have the resources to gather more information, the expertise to process it, and the strategic thinking to make use of it.

THE MARKETPLACE GETS BROADER AND FASTER

To give you an example of how the availability of greatly increased information changes the marketplace you're working in, I'm first going to have to lay down another Law and also put a little more math up on my imaginary chalkboard. For those of you still trying to wrap your head around that "2 × 2 × 2 × 2 × 2 × 2 × 2 × 2 × 2 × 2 = 1,024" deal, I apologize, but I'll try to make it as simple as possible—really!

Metcalfe's Law—another great invention—says: *The value of a network is the square of its number of participants.* To answer the question you probably have about that statement ("Huh?"), let me give an example. If you have ten members in your business or social network, the value of the network is 10 x 10 (the square of ten), or 100. If the network increases to one hundred members, its value becomes 100 × 100, or 10,000. You now have ten times as many people in the network, but the network itself has now become *one hundred* times as valuable. That exponential increase, following Metcalfe's Law, is a result of the larger number of interconnections you get with a larger network and the greater opportunities to exchange ideas, abilities, and information.

To get more specific: Let's say you have some rookie baseball cards from the 1980s you want to sell, and you're in the market to buy some rare collectible Beanie Babies of the early '90s. (I'm not judging anybody here, just making up an example.) You need some information about the marketplace out there: a potential buyer and a potential seller. You look first among the ten members (network value = 100) of your neighborhood association. What are the chances that network will provide you with the information you need? Not that good. Then you go to the hundred people (network value = 10,000) who read the bulletin board in your community center. You might have some luck there, but very possibly not.

Now let's say you go to a big network with a huge amount of information—like eBay. With 20 million regular users, the value of that network, according to Metcalfe's Law, comes out to 20 million squared. My calculator doesn't go that high, but that's got to be a number up near a gazillion. With such a network, the information you now have available means it's possible that you won't just find someone interested in old baseball cards in general, but even someone who desperately wants your 1982 Cal Ripken, Jr. card. You also have a good chance of finding someone who can sell you that special 1993 Sparkle Pink Pony Beanie Baby (again, not judging).

As with most things in life, there's a flip side. In a bigger marketplace with more information, five other people might be out there with you, ready to sell *their* 1982 Ripken card. Some of them may be willing to sell their product at a lower price, faster, and charge less for shipping. The information that's helping you is helping everyone else as well. You've got to move fast to keep up.

From "Up to the Minute" to "Up to the Second"

Businesses now require more detailed information to make decisions. One example of this development is the method movie studios often use to test a sample audience's response to upcoming films.

In test screenings of the past, cards would be passed out to audience members, who would mark what they liked and didn't like in the movie they'd just seen. After some advances in technology, and greater competition in the movie business, audience members now are frequently asked to turn a dial as they watch the film—one way for "fun, interesting, exciting" and the other for "get on with it already." (A similar method, by the way, is sometimes used by pollsters and political consultants to assess the public reaction to a candidate's speech or debate performance.) The second-by-second responses can be interpreted to help decide if certain scenes should be cut, or just edited down a few seconds, in order to create the most audience-friendly product possible.

WE WANT CHANGE AND WE WANT IT NOW

Let's be honest about this. We can't blame all the change we see in the world on advances in technology or on a glut of information available all the time. What's really at the bottom of all of this change, of course, begins with that third letter in the word TIP: *People.*

It's obvious that people cause change in one sense: they're the ones creating all those marvelously faster microchips and other technological goodies. Computers don't create new and better versions of themselves—at least not yet. People are also the ones adding to our store of information, as they post a blog about their pet cats, or favorite television show, and push the number of web pages out there up into the billions. So people are indeed the creators of changes in technology and information.

But there's a more important angle to look at here, especially from the point of view of your business. People not only create the elements that make change happen, but they also are the source of the *need, desire, and market* for change. People buy things, they use things, they expect things, and they raise the bar in terms of their expectations every single day. Can't you see how the bar is being raised on you too? It's being raised in terms of what your customers want, when they want it, how they want it, and what they are willing to pay for it.

You might ask if it is possible to lower people's expectations. That would make life for your business easier, wouldn't it? Unfortunately, that's basically impossible to do. The reason why is that it's not just some unreasonable "they" out there who are raising the bar of expectations. It's *everybody* who is doing so, including you and me. We all want things faster, cheaper, with better service, and of higher quality. When it comes to who is demanding that businesses raise the bar, it's like a line from the old *Pogo* comic strip: "We have met the enemy and he is us."

We can't have it both ways. We can't have it one way as a consumer and the other way as a businessperson. Being able to buy a high-definition, flat screen television that's 20 percent larger and 20 percent cheaper than the one we saw three months ago?

Fantastic. Having our own customers insist on a similar increase in quality and reduction in cost? Not so fantastic.

But we can't walk out the door of our own company at night wanting to buy the latest, greatest, smallest, largest, fastest, cheapest products and not expect that desire to have the same sort of impact on what we do and how we do it. Regardless of your particular job, your profession, or your industry, one thing remains true:

The bar goes up.

Another driving force of change related to people is simply this: There are more of us on the earth every day. It took a few million years for the world's population to get to the 6.5 billion people we have today. It's said that at the current pace, we will add the next 6.5 billion people in just fifty years. We add a city the size of Las Vegas to this earth's population ... every single day. That's more than 1 million every day. And together they will cause a rise in competition and expectations every day as well.

The bar goes up.

Once expectations are raised, once technology makes its impact, we can't expect that there to be any turning back. Things will only go faster.

Let me give you an example. I visited the house of some friends of mine recently. As I walked in the front door, I saw their four-year-old daughter playing on the computer. I went over and watched her for a few minutes. She's got the mouse. She's clicking, she's double clicking. She's opening programs, she's closing programs. She's loading CDs, opening games, playing games, winning games. The sound is going. The graphics are going.

I stood there in amazement, and, looking down at her happy face, I said, "Wow, Jennifer, you are really good at this." She smiled back up at me and said, "Yeah ... and think how good I will be when I'm able to read!"

The bar goes up ... *and it's four-year-olds who are doing it!*

CHANGE IS INEVITABLE ... AND UNPREDICTABLE

Let's take ourselves back to 1965 for a minute. That's when Gordon Moore so brilliantly predicted that computer chips would double in capacity every two years or even less, leading to the exponential growth in technology that drives much of the change we see today. How do you think people that year would expect the world to have changed by now, the early stages of the twenty-first century?

Back then, it had only been a few years since the first man had gone into orbit around the Earth and would only be a few more before one man took a small step onto the moon. If you asked typical Mr. or Mrs. 1965 (I don't think the word "Ms." had been invented yet) to predict what would develop over the next forty years, he or she might talk of weekend trips to the moon, the development of interstellar overdrive (whatever the heck that is), and everyone wearing those cool matching silver jumpsuits with the logos on the left front. People wouldn't need to worry about running out of fossil fuels, Mr. or Mrs. 1965 would assume, because surely by this new century they'd have invented some great power source so you could run your car—sorry, *jet* car—on tap water.

Things haven't quite worked out that way. I don't know about you, but I'm still waiting for that flying jet pack I was counting on getting someday after seeing one in a James Bond movie as a kid. As for rocketing toward the stars—well, the total number of people who had left the Earth's orbit (all of them moon-ward bound) by 1972 was twenty-four. And the total number today is ... still twenty-four. That cheap new energy source hasn't arrived yet either, as you must realize every time you see how high the price spins up to whenever you fill your car with gas. And instead of being concerned about running out of fossil fuels, we're more worried today whether burning them will overheat the planet first. Many of the changes that might have been expected just haven't arrived.

Unexpected Developments

Now let's consider all the things that *have* changed over the last forty years that few people would have anticipated back in those Space Age days. Many of these developments involve personal technology and communication. Phone answering machines—a rarity back then—have become so ubiquitous that hearing a phone ring more than four times is now taken as a sign that something is wrong. Cell phones have become so common that we're no longer surprised to see people walking down the street talking to themselves; instead, we're surprised and annoyed if we can't get in touch with and talk to someone at any hour of the day.

Forty years ago, when few offices had computers, few people would have imagined that someday every home would have one (or two, or three, or four). And who would have expected that these computers would shrink in a few years from ones that bulkily covered a desk to ones that could fit in a briefcase, and finally in one hand? The absolute need for a computer is now taken for granted, as is the ability to contact anyone anywhere anytime via e-mail. We also now can't imagine not being able to, within a few seconds, pull up on our computer screen a listing of all the houses for sale in our town, or our favorite baseball player's on-base percentage, updated after his last at-bat.

The simple fact is this: Change *in general* is predictable and unavoidable, in that it will unquestionably occur. But change *in particular* is impossible to see ahead of time with any clarity. One reason for this is that people predict future change based on their present—and really, without the ability to take a quick scouting trip in a time machine, what else *could* they base it on? People in the mid-1960s saw rapid developments in space travel, and they figured that was where change was headed. Innovations headed their way in personal computing and communication were harder to notice.

Let's imagine that you are trying to predict what will change in the next ten or twenty years in the way you do business, or in your daily life, or in the newest technologies. You'd probably base your predictions on the trends and developments you see today. As in: "Well, my current cell phone is smaller than the one I had two years ago, so I guess cell phones are going to get really, really, *really* small." There's a good chance you'd be right, at least in the short term. But what if at some point another form of communication replaces the cell phone? Could you possibly know well ahead of time what that will be?

WHAT YOU CAN—AND CAN'T—ANTICIPATE

"Now, wait a minute," you might be saying. "Of *course* I can't predict major changes in technology and society. But how about the smaller everyday changes that affect my business? That's what I'm really concerned about. Can't I anticipate those and prepare myself for them in advance?"

Good question. (I'm glad you asked.) Yes, some changes in your business life can be anticipated. But let's go back to the items I asked you to jot down at the beginning of the chapter, all the things that had changed in your business and your work life over the past two years. (You did jot them down, didn't you? If you didn't, just take a minute to think about those changes in your organization. I'll wait right here.)

All right, now take a look at the changes over that period. In a general way, many of them have probably been predictable. You knew there would be shifts in markets, personnel, policies, and so on. But in most cases the specifics of the changes were pretty much impossible to predict. Did you really know ahead of time which important client you would lose (or gain) . . . which key member of your team would leave for another company . . . which new competitor would pose the strongest threat . . . and so on? And what about those changes that *really* threw you for a loop, like when your organization got a new leader, or new ownership, or a new location.

Change is unpredictable. And this fact leads to one of the most crucial reasons why you need to be reading this book in the first place:

> **You can't know *which* changes will occur, so your most valuable skill is being able to master *any* changes that do.**

I said earlier that in the New Business Reality we face today, your greatest career asset is your ability to be a change agent in your organization. Knowing how to deal with the expected is no longer enough. You need to learn how to master the inevitable, yet unpredictable, change you and your organization will face.

WHICH CHANGES REALLY MATTER

All the talk in this chapter about developments in computers, space flight, cell phones, and other technological advances leads to one important point: The most significant changes are those involving everyday things, and the way we live, work, and communicate with one another. Grand achievements in exploration and discovery are one thing, but the development of the restaurant drive-through or eBay has changed people's lives more than the Apollo program ever will. Even if you can't predict which changes the future will bring, you can get an idea of which areas of change are most worth your attention. And the most important changes to worry about are those that involve how you relate to and interact with your colleagues, others in your field, and—most crucially—your customers.

A TYPICAL ORGANIZATION—LIKE YOURS— DEALS WITH CHANGE

In a number of chapters throughout this book, I'll tell a story of the people working in an ordinary business dealing with an aspect of change. Some of the business books I've seen lately tell their stories through little tales involving mice or penguins or whatever. With the exception of a parable about a group of monkeys (and who doesn't love monkeys?!), the stories given here will involve people, and will—I hope—be similar to many of your own experiences. I've just never found that when faced with a difficult situation in business it is very helpful to ask, "Now what would an aardvark do?"

I will also try to be specific about the challenges, feelings, and responses people have in the situations this company finds itself in. Some details will be left fairly general so that you can relate to what's described no matter what you do in your business or organization. As a first step, let's name our typical little company. Sometimes, imaginary companies in business books are given names like "The Acme Widget Company."

That sounds a little too fake to me, as the only company named Acme I've ever seen is the one that sells ineffectual products to Wile E. Coyote. And even though there really are things called "widgets" now—it's a kind of web-based application—the word still sounds something like "thingamajig" to me. So let's call our company Forest Associates. It's a financial services company of about fifty people dealing with all the issues faced by a small- to medium-sized organization today—sales, customer service, competition, maintaining a productive and effective workforce, and more.

In the hundreds of workshops and training sessions I've held at companies over the years, I've found one thing to be true. Organizations dealing with change face specific challenges that can vary greatly—depending on the company's field, location, management structure, size, etc.—but the experiences most groups of employees go through are more similar than not. In following the good people at Forest Associates, and in the rest of the examples, exercises, and tips you'll see in this book, I'll try to show what it's like for real people to cope with—and triumph over—the real, unavoidable change they face every day.

SUMMING UP

At the end of each chapter—as in right now—I'll give you a few bullet points you should be sure to carry with you before moving on to the next chapter. Here's a quick summary of Chapter 1:

- The amount and pace of change businesses face today is much greater than it was even ten years ago.
- Change is not a product of decisions within companies. It's an inescapable result of faster technological progress, more and more information to process, and—most of all—people demanding products faster, cheaper, and of higher quality.
- The specifics of change are unpredictable, so you and your organization need to develop your skills for mastering any change that may come along.

02

FOUR GUARANTEES

When you consider the role that coping with change is going to play in your career and your organization, the specifics will certainly vary quite a lot and, as I mentioned above, be impossible to predict. But there are several general characteristics of change that are sure to be true. In fact, I'll guarantee them. Then, after describing them, I'll define what I call the New Business Reality, and how it has been created by these four inevitable attributes of change today.

IT'S NOT GOING AWAY

Here's the first thing I can guarantee:

Change is here to stay.

You probably could guess I'd guarantee that. Change won't just go away. For anyone who is waiting for things to go back to the way they were in the good old days . . . keep waiting. It's just not going to happen.

If your organization is at all like those I've worked with in recent years, you've had the following experience. Your organization goes through a major reorganization or system implementation. After all the hard work, uncertainty, and stumbling blocks, everyone heaves a sigh of relief when it's done. "Whew! Good thing that's over with! Won't have to deal with that for another five years!" At least, not until the next reorganization or new system comes along two years . . . twelve months . . . or six months later. Today, it's not even months before you can expect the next change—it's days or even hours! Soon enough, we learn that change is not an exception or a temporary phase to be gotten through. It's a simple fact of life.

IT'S NOT GOING TO SLOW DOWN

Here's the second thing I can guarantee:

The pace of change will increase.

You know the rapid change that I've been talking about? I'm sorry to tell to you, but that pace is the slowest that you will ever experience! Not only will all this change stuff not go away, but the pace will do nothing but increase.

Consider this: In the 1950s, most companies faced just one organizational change in the entire decade. With just one change in the decade, companies had several years to plan for, talk about, and implement a change. That left a few years to assimilate the change, work out the bugs, and make it part of what they did on a day-to-day basis. Plenty of time to prepare, and to recover, with a few years left over to enjoy that antique state known as "stability" before the next change came along.

Moving on to the 1960s, companies saw an average of two major organizational changes per decade. Not so much time was left anymore to prepare for, recover from, and enjoy the benefits of a change. In the 1970s, three major organizational changes within ten years was typical. The time of preparation and recovery was down to about two years. By the 1980s, you could expect an organizational change every eighteen months or so. One key point to make here: The changes during these periods were not necessarily different *types* of changes. Throughout, companies were facing downsizing, mergers and acquisitions, restructuring and reengineering, reorganizations, and so on. It's just that the *pace* of changes had increased so much.

Look at the 1990s, the new century, and beyond . . . now the changes come in waves. They come two or three at a time. Now, we're not only changing the technology, the process, and the system. We're also changing my role, your role, and we are trying to reengineer ourselves all at the same time. Faster and faster.

IT'S NOT GOING TO BE EASY

Here's a third guarantee:

This change won't be trouble-free.

Inevitably, each change will bring at least a measure of problems, challenges, and frustrations. People have an understandable tendency to think that these problems mean the change was bad, or that it is being mismanaged. They take a step back and say, "See, I *told* you that was a bad idea." Wrong. The trouble that accompanies a change doesn't necessarily mean it was a bad idea. All the challenges are simply a natural dynamic of the change process.

One reason the challenges that accompany every change can be so discouraging is that we are so often told they don't exist. How often have you seen someone stand in front of a group before a change is implemented—or perhaps you've stood in front of a group yourself—with the message that everything will be fine? "Here's the change, here's what we have to do . . . but don't worry, it will all be okay. This new policy/software/supervisor/management structure will improve things so much you'll wonder how we lived without it before. No problem."

managing *UP*

LEARNING FROM MISTAKES

Everyone's going to make mistakes during the process of change. Just make sure that you learn from them! Take the time to write out a brief (that's a key word here: *brief*) explanation of what went wrong, how you'd do things differently, and what you've learned. The human mind has a wonderful capacity for forgetting its mistakes quickly. You want to move past your mistakes, but you *really* don't want to repeat them.

There *will* be problems, frustrations, and starts and stops that go along with the change. Pretending they don't exist will only make things harder. In the chapter that follows, we'll discuss why every change has at least a temporary negative effect on the function of your organization. After that, we'll move on to explore why resistance to change is a perfectly natural response. And then, in the rest of the book, we'll discover how you can minimize the problems and resistance that come with change. After that, the next time you have to introduce a change you won't say, "No problem," but instead: "Here are the problems, and here is how we will get past them to achieve something bigger and better than before."

IT'S NOT SOMEONE ELSE'S PROBLEM

Douglas Adams's *The Hitchhiker's Guide to the Galaxy* is a series of novels full of delightfully wacky British humor. In one of the books in the series, there's a scene where, oddly enough, a spaceship appears on the playing field during a cricket match. Even more oddly, none of the spectators notice it. The narrator explains to us that the reason no one in the crowd sees the spaceship is because it is an "SEP"—*Someone Else's Problem*. And one aspect of human nature is that everything we consider to be "someone else's problem" is basically invisible to us. We have enough problems of our own to keep track of, to worry about events that don't concern us.

I mentioned earlier that many people like to blame their bosses for the changes in their workplace, when change is actually something inherent in business today. Just as people may try to pin the responsibility for change on someone in their organization, they also may believe that the problem of dealing with change is not something *they* have to worry about. They may get to the point where they don't notice there's a problem to be dealt with at all. Instead, people in this state of denial think that if they just keep working hard, doing the same things they've always been doing, that somehow everything will turn out fine. Change is "someone else's problem," and it is not even visible on their radar screen.

Well, dealing with change *isn't* someone else's problem. It's a problem everyone in business—including those at all levels of your organization—must face today. And when it comes to facing up to change in your organization, here's a fourth guarantee I can make:

You are accountable for dealing with change.

Not only are you accountable for your own job and your own productivity, you are also accountable in your role as a change agent. You are expected to do what you are used to doing, and you are also expected to make this new change work. Every single time that you accept compensation, you are agreeing to that accountability. You are paid to deliver a job, as employees have always been, but you are also paid to figure out a better way of doing it. A more effective way. A safer way. A less costly way. Businesses and organizations need to be able to adapt to change in order to survive today, and the more responsible your position is, the more you are personally accountable for that adaptability. And by the way, when I say business, that means people. And people means you!

GOODBYE TO STABILITY AND SECURITY

Before we define the New Business Reality of our daily workplace, let's take a look at the *Old* Business Reality that preceded it.

Anyone entering the business world twenty or thirty years ago faced a very different set of challenges from what we see today. It's clear that the *mastery* required for success in business has changed. In the Old Reality, businesses were more likely to have clearly defined roles for employees, with set tasks and well-defined expectations. As an employee, you were given the opportunity to master the job, as well as the company's system. You first went to school, learned a set of skills, got a job at the bottom rung of the career ladder, and then came in and practiced those skills every single day. If you worked hard enough, you got really good at this. Pretty soon, you became the best THIS that your company ever had. Plaques hanging on the wall someplace proclaimed that you were the THIS OF THE YEAR five years in a row.

Companies and industries always had change, but in the Old Reality they also had time to get through them. Occasionally you'd have to go from an old system to a new system. It took you a couple of extra nights and a weekend or two, but soon you were as good at the new system as you were at the old system. You mastered it.

In exchange for this mastery, companies rewarded their employees with security, or at least with a good prospect of a job over the long term. For meeting a company's expectations, an employee could in turn expect steadily rising responsibility and pay, and possibly even a reasonable pension at the end of a career. (A pension? Really? Now when's the last time you even heard that word?)

Where did the customer fit into all this? Well, if a company and its employees met a customer's expectations, and if they established a good relationship and solid reputation with a customer, they could expect some loyalty from that customer in return. Consumers have always shopped around and been interested in trying new things, but just as the relationship between companies and employees used to be more stable, so did the one between a company and its customers. We might define the Old Business Reality as follows:

1. Companies set clear expectations within well-defined jobs.
2. Employees met those expectations, and they were rewarded with stability and security.
3. Customers rewarded the companies that met their expectations with loyalty and continued business.

Sounds like one big happy family, doesn't it? Yes, I know, I know ... there's a lot I'm leaving out of this pretty picture. Companies—and their employees—have always dealt with downturns, layoffs, and all sorts of problems. My point is not that business functioned this way for every company, employee, and customer back in the Old Business Reality. It's that this was the *goal* back then, the way things were *supposed* to run. Being a successful company meant that you operated under this model.

DEFINING THE NEW BUSINESS REALITY

Remember all that faster and faster change—in business, society, and technology—that we've been talking about? (I certainly hope so.) The important result of all that change is that the Old Business Reality has been tossed out the window, to be replaced by the New Business Reality we face today.

Companies and organizations no longer can stand still, simply absorbing an occasional small change in their system. They have to keep moving. The tasks they required of their employees even

23

a few years ago may not be what are required today. In all this change, companies also can't promise their employees the loyalty and security of the past. Employees, in turn, can't rely on the skills they learned in the past to see them through. In today's environment, as soon as you master a system, what happens? A newer system comes along. No longer can employees simply master the *job*. And while you can't ever master the *change*, we have to shift our focus. Now, your value to an organization is not in knowing how to do something better, cheaper, and faster than anyone else. It lies equally in an ability and willingness to change from what you are doing today to what your organization needs you to do tomorrow. This is different from the old days of: "Teach me a set of skills, let me practice them every day, leave me alone for the rest of my career." It's not necessarily better or worse . . . just different.

managing DOWN

INFORMATION OVERLOAD

Your staff is going to be challenged by the immense amount of new information that they'll have to process. Keep in mind that learning styles are individual. Some people learn better by reading a manual on their own, some learn better through demonstrations in groups. If you can, present the new information in ways that fit your staff's learning styles—so that they can learn more quickly and efficiently.

How about the customers? The value that your business brings to your customers no longer lies just in doing what you do better, faster, and cheaper than anyone else—though that is still essential. It lies equally in your ability as an organization to change from what you are doing to what they (the marketplace) wants you to do. You can no longer expect customers to stay with you out of simple loyalty. You can, however, work to change quickly enough to meet their evolving needs and desires.

The change from Old to New Business Reality has brought with it insecurity and instability. We can define the New Business Reality as follows:

1. Companies are faced with constant change, and they spend much of their energy simply in keeping up.
2. Unable to rely on a stable working environment, employees must set their own career expectations, and they are rewarded to the extent they serve as change agents.
3. Customers continually search for those companies most attuned to their needs in the present and in the future.

This is the new business atmosphere we're working in. We have to set our own expectations to fit this new reality and not count on being told what to do and how to do it. We've got to figure out where all this change is headed and work on the qualities, skills, and behaviors that will help us be valuable, marketable, and employable in a radically different environment.

SUMMING UP

- One thing is guaranteed: Change is here to stay.
- A second guarantee: The pace of change will do nothing but increase.
- A third: All of this change won't be trouble free.
- And a fourth: You are accountable for dealing with change.
- In the business environment of the past, stability and security were the goals companies strove for and could sometimes offer to their employees.
- In the New Business Reality, employees must set their own expectations, and they must work to enable their companies to change, to constantly meet their customer's evolving needs.

03

MORE CHANGE =
LESS PRODUCTIVITY

In the Introduction to this book, recall that I made the following direct statement:

When you change how you do things, your productivity always goes down *initially*.

You might have read that and thought it could be *sort of* true: Change does have its problems, so you'd suppose it can cause a bit of drag on productivity, even if things in your overall organization carry on well enough. The point of this chapter is to demonstrate that the above statement really *is* true, and that changes in the way you do things have effects that reach all the way through your organization. Adding these effects together, you'll find that any really significant change will bring down your productivity *overall* at least temporarily. Smaller changes won't have as big an impact, but they will have measurable negative effects of their own. Once you understand how change harms productivity—the very thing it is often intended to improve—the task of learning to master change will seem even more urgent.

QUALITY AND SPEED GO DOWN

With any substantial change, there will be a drop in productivity. I'll give you an illustration of just how that can happen.

Find two blank pieces of paper (maybe two of those I asked you to pull out in Chapter 1) and a pen or a pencil. On one of those sheets of paper, take exactly sixty seconds and sign your first and last name as many times as you can, as legibly as possible. It should be just like signing your name to a check or a letter. One difference: you should make sure that someone who didn't know your name would at least have a shot at figuring out all the letters you write each time. Take a look at your watch. All right, ready, set . . . and begin.

Once sixty seconds have passed, it's time for the old "Pens and pencils down, please." (This is one place where I wish I was making an audio book instead of a paper one; it would be great to include sixty seconds of silence here followed by the sound of a timer buzzer going off.) So, how did you do? Whatever number you reached, don't worry about it—this is not a competition. I fully expect that anyone with a name like, say, Ed Mays is going to post a higher score than Elizabeth Williams-Martinson would.

And now, to make clear the whole point of the exercise—yes, there really is one—take the other sheet of the paper, put your pen or pencil into your other hand, the one you don't normally write with, and get ready to sign your name for sixty seconds as before. Yes, that's what I said, the *other* hand. And no, you can't practice a signature or two with this unfamiliar hand—just look at your watch and get going.

Time's up! How did you do this time? Not as well, I'm pretty sure. In the interest of full disclosure, my own scores when I tried this exercise were seventeen signatures with my regular hand, going down to seven with my other hand. And those seven "Karl Schoemers" with my off hand were a little shaky, to say the least. Looking at their wavering curves, I got flashbacks to afternoons spent in the second grade learning how to write in cursive. Mrs. Martin definitely wouldn't have accepted the poor quality of work I produced here.

What can we say about the change from working with your familiar hand to the other one? As you were writing the second set of signatures, I'm willing to bet that you discovered:

1. You felt less comfortable and confident, especially at first.
2. You had to work harder and concentrate more, because you couldn't accomplish the task as naturally and unthinkingly as you normally could.
3. You had to try to quickly ascend the learning curve, so that you could move on from your first tentative attempt to something at least marginally better.
4. A little voice inside you was wondering, "Now *why* exactly do I have to do it this new way?"
5. The measurable *quantity* of your output decreased from your previous effort.
6. The visible *quality* of your output worsened as well.

The above six points apply to this somewhat trivial handwriting exercise, but much more importantly, they also perfectly describe what happens whenever you and the people in your organization have to change to do something in a new, unfamiliar way.

When you first implement a new system/software/structure in your business, you always feel less certain about what you're doing than you did with the "old way" (point #1). Working on autopilot is no longer an option, so you have to put in more effort and concentration (#2). In a fast-paced business environment, you don't have the time to slowly and carefully incorporate the new change. You have to hit the ground running and catch on quickly—maybe not in sixty seconds, but as quickly as possible (#3). Along with the difficulties in incorporating a change, you naturally feel a little resistance to the idea of making a change at all (#4)—something we'll explore in more detail in Chapter 4. (By the way, the answer to the question in #4 for this particular exercise is: *Because I told you to do it.* Someday, when you write your own book on businesses adapting to change, you can tell readers to do all sorts of crazy things, too.) And isn't that the way change sometimes comes to us? "This is what we are going to do . . . now go do it this way."

The heart of the matter here is found in points #5 and #6. The initial drop in quantity and quality caused by a major change affects every organization, and it is something that you must learn to minimize as much as possible.

managing *DOWN*

ATTENTION TO DETAILS

Setting a faster pace doesn't mean letting key things go. Make sure you identify and satisfy the critical needs of your customers and/or organization before you start choosing what to do and what not to do.

I can foresee one objection to the analogy I'm making. It might go something like this: "Hold on a minute. I can understand how quantity and quality will suffer when you make a drastic change like switching your writing hand. Things will *always* get worse if you switch to an inferior way of doing things. But what if we're changing to a better system/software/structure? Shouldn't that improve things right away?"

Let's think about that for a minute. Have you ever started using a new software program and found that *from the very first minute* you understood how to use it just as well or better than the one you were used to? Have you ever changed your phone system and had things work perfectly on the first day, without any hesitation, hiccups, or resorting to the manual? Maybe you've been lucky enough to have such immediate, painless change once or twice, but it's really not the norm, is it?

The majority of changes may help you in the long run. And sometimes you can get to the long run more quickly than other times. That's the whole point here—moving as quickly as possible to reach the point where the change no longer causes you to do things worse than before. Until you get there, you'll be putting in *more* concentration and energy to achieve *less* quantity and lower quality. That's a deadly combination for you and your business.

CHANGE SLOWS EFFICIENCY—DROP BY DROP

Let's visit Forest Associates, that typical, if imaginary, medium-sized company I mentioned in Chapter 1, and consider an example of how change always puts a drag on an organization's efficiency *at least for a while*. To do this, we don't need to move the main office to Saskatoon, Saskatchewan, or swap all the PC computers for Macs. No, let's just replace the office's coffeemaker.

Up to now, our little office has gotten along with one of those two-burner-ring coffeemakers—one burner with a pot down below where the coffee is made, and a second one on top, heating up a pot one-quarter full of coffee of unknown age. No one likes the coffee very much, and everybody grumbles about having to make more every hour and clean the pots at the end of the day. As for having a choice of coffees—well, that pot with the orange top might have decaf, but no one's really sure.

Good news! Our kind and generous management has decided to replace our ancient coffeemaker with a shiny and new hot-beverage *system*: the Caffeinator Turbo 3000. From now on, you'll just place your cup under a spout, drop in a packet labeled with the drink of your choice, and push a button. Fifteen seconds later, you'll have a steaming cup of Mountain Colombian. Or perhaps

Mocha Cappuccino, Vermont Cocoa, or Decaf Venezuelan Latte. It'll be just like going to Starbucks, only without having to shell out four bucks or figure out the difference between "tall," "grande," and "venti."

As it happens, our clever management is not installing the system just to be kind. (You probably guessed that.) Their hope is that the new system will cut down the time spent making coffee—or running to Starbucks to avoid making coffee—and that the end result will be happier, java-fueled employees who will work more quickly and productively. Our new coffee-making gizmo might even help to impress clients coming in for meetings, or job candidates we want to hire.

Eventually, the Caffeinator Turbo 3000 may do all those things. But for now—for today, and maybe the rest of the week—this change meant to increase productivity is going to decrease it just a little. Why? Because, no matter how much time people used to spend each day making coffee or complaining about it, they are going to spend more time today and over the next few days reading the new instructions, trying out the system, discussing it with colleagues, and so on. They may even have to go get a mop once or twice when someone has trouble getting the order of "insert packet–put cup under nozzle–press button" correct. We also have to add in the time it took for the facility manager to evaluate the various coffee-machine vendors, get the go-ahead and the paperwork through accounting, and set up the time for the new installation. Add it all up, and you can see that even if it's only a small impact, every change in the way you do things will have *some* effect on efficiency.

CHANGE TAKES TIME AND ENERGY

When you get to the parts of your business more important than how you make coffee, change will be accompanied by the greatest drag on productivity yet invented. *Meetings!* You'll need meetings to discuss what other changes to make down the road, another one to finalize the imminent change, a wider meeting to inform other departments of the change, and follow-up meetings to see how the change is working out.

Even a fifteen-minute "gather 'round everybody" to explain a new policy comes with its own cost in productivity. If twenty people are involved, that brief confab adds up to five hours of paid work time that your organization will never get back. (I'll pause here a minute if you want to check my math.) By the way, that exponential two to the tenth power I mentioned back in Chapter 1 can also be applied to the number of meetings I see in organizations every day.

To continue . . . Your organization will have to spend time and energy to decide upon, broadcast, and evaluate every change. But most changes will also require additional effort to implement. Employees may need to be trained in new software or procedures. Customers may need to be informed of the change in your operation, either through advertising or direct contact. Managers will have to spend more time in coaching, encouraging, and just plain *selling* the new change. With all the time and effort it takes to change, it's no surprise that the initial announcement of every change is greeted with something other than wild enthusiasm.

CHANGE CONFLICTS WITH WHAT YOU'RE ALREADY DOING

Change may suck up your time and energy, but at least while you're implementing a change, your company will ease up on the other tasks and goals it requires of you and your department, right?

Umm . . . won't it?

Sorry to say it, but I think you already know the answer: No, your company won't. You may wish you had a supremely understanding boss who, when introducing a change said something like: "We know that doing this will require some adjustments and a lot of hard work, so it's okay if you don't make your quarterly numbers, or file all your reports, or get all your regular work done for a while." Maybe you *do* have such a boss, though in the hundreds of organizations I've worked with I don't think I've met one myself. And this is perfectly understandable. Companies and organizations make changes to perform current tasks better and to improve the end results. When that's the goal, no one thinks it's acceptable to slack off on anything already being done now. In a more competitive, fast-changing business environment, it would be surprising and even dangerous if they did.

Whether those in charge of an organization accept it or not, though, the effort you put into making a change has a trickle-down effect on everything else you do. An hour spent in a meeting learning a new system could have been an hour on the phone helping several longtime customers. A daylong retreat establishing your "new corporate culture" after a buy-out could have been a day of wrapping up all that paperwork you need to complete. Once you finish the meeting or retreat, you can be sure the customer issues or paperwork will still be patiently waiting, only now you will have even less time to deal with them properly.

This is the ripple effect of making a change. First, the particular task you are doing differently now may be more difficult, at least for a while. And then everything in your work life becomes just a bit more squeezed—something that is hard to even imagine, I know—and has to take a temporary backseat to the new, unavoidable change.

LIMIT THE DEPTH AND DURATION

Earlier on, I mentioned that two words you'd be hearing later would be *depth* and *duration*. Well, here they are! When I lead workshops on managing change, I tell the participants that there will be a one-question quiz at the end of the day, and that the answer will be "Limit the depth and duration." Now that you have the answer, let's do things in that backward way they do on *Jeopardy!* and see if you know the question:

Answer: Limit the depth and duration.

Question: What do we need to do about the inevitable drop that change causes in our company's productivity?

Because you can't prevent a drop in productivity, you must manage both its depth and its duration. Make it as shallow and short as possible. Now, I've stated that this drop in overall productivity is an unavoidable companion of any significant change. And the previous sections in this chapter spell out some of the reasons why:

The way that doing something differently hurts speed and quality

The time and effort needed to implement a change

The trickle-down effect change has on the parts of your operation that haven't changed

Still, in my workshops, whenever I get to this "depth-and-duration" part, it's not uncommon for someone to say that change doesn't really cause a drop of productivity in their own operation. Maybe in someone *else's* department, but not in theirs. And maybe you've thought the same thing. Sure, change has its problems, but can't we just push a little harder and get through it?

If you think change doesn't hurt your productivity, you're not looking at the whole picture. Consider what happens in a business during times of change. See how much overtime people put in. Whether they officially document it or not, it's there. Look at the work people take home. Look at the frustration level of employees, gritting their teeth trying to cope with all of this change.

All this stress and extra effort may mean that the department or organization manages to hit their quarterly numbers or not fall behind on their absolutely essential work. But this extra effort cannot be kept up forever. People will burn out, important tasks will be postponed in favor of making sure the change is accomplished, and so on. If you have to work a lot harder to get the same result, your productivity has gone down. The solution: Get through the change as quickly as possible. When it comes to the drop in productivity . . . yup, *limit the depth and duration.*

Reaching a Whole Other Level

Here's another reason why you need to limit the depth and duration of the negative effects of change. Even when you're able to return to your pre-change productivity level, your job is not done. After all, the entire point of the change is to improve things. Yes, after you limit the depth and duration of the drop in productivity, you need to raise productivity *higher than it ever was before.* The status quo is just not good enough.

Remember: We're not talking about "this" or "the" change. What we're really talking about is increasing your ability to manage quickly and effectively through all change. Because it's not going to stop or go away.

What happens, then, if you get mired in the most awkward part of a change—and the next change occurs? Where does the drop in productivity begin for the next change? It begins at the lower, unacceptable level of the drop from the first one. Oh, wait . . . here comes yet another change. And one more following closely behind it. If you don't recover from changes as quickly as possible, the graph of your productivity will resemble a staircase—one heading right down into the cellar. You need to equip people with the skills, knowledge, and tools necessary to navigate rapidly through each drop in productivity and come out higher each time.

MISMANAGED CHANGE BRINGS MORE CHANGE

Let me give you an example of what can happen if the productivity downturn following a change is not managed properly—and just as importantly, if it is not *understood* properly. Your organization says that you need to make a change. Right-size, downsize, merge, acquire, restructure, reengineer, reorganize, resystemize—whatever. "Come on everyone, let's make this change! It will improve things dramatically!" And then your organization makes the change without seriously trying to manage the inevitable drop in productivity, without equipping people with the tools to do so. In fact, the management of your organization doesn't even know there *will* be a productivity drop caused by the change. (I guess they haven't read this book.)

Fast-forward to nine months from now. Your management team takes a look at the latest figures and says: "Now hold on a minute. Not only have we not been able to see the improvement in productivity we expected from that change, but productivity is actually *below* where it was when we started." What lesson are they going to draw from this? Are they going to think that they've mismanaged the change and not gotten through the change as quickly as they should? (Let me remind you again that they haven't read this book.) No, they are going to draw a very different lesson from the numbers they see:

The change didn't work!

So what do you need to do now? Change again, of course! So you change again ... you change up, you change down, you re-restructure, you re-reengineer, you re-reorganize. You're starting this new change from a slightly lower level of productivity. You also are starting it with employees who are still worn out from the most recent change and who will have less faith and trust in management after being told to reverse direction so soon. So the new change will be implemented with less energy and commitment than the last one. And, for all you know, the last change might actually have been the *right* change—it was just mismanaged and never given enough of a chance to help productivity in the long run. With all of this going against it, the chances that this new change will take you where you want to go look slim. After it doesn't, what will happen next? You guessed it—yet another change.

The bottom line is that understanding the need to mitigate the depth and duration of the productivity drop following each and every change can actually become part of your competitive advantage. How quickly, smoothly, and successfully you move yourself and your organization through this process can make or break your success in handling constant, complex change being brought to us by a volatile marketplace.

SUMMING UP

- Whenever you do something in a new way, you'll do it slower and with lower quality, at least at first.
- If you haven't learned to effectively manage through change, the time and effort your organization puts into a change is a drain on your overall efficiency.
- The elements of your organization that are changing take away needed energy from those that are staying the same.
- Productivity *will* drop during a change—limit the depth and duration!
- Mismanaged change (marked by slow, unequipped employees, or lack of attention to depth and duration) leaves you worse off than before and results in even more change.

04

RESISTANCE IS NATURAL

Our general inability to recognize transformative change when we
see it is legendary—almost a cliché. From, "It'll never fly, Wilbur,"
to Thomas Watson's famous prediction that "... there is a world
market for maybe five computers" (and he was the chairman of
IBM!), even the experts have a pretty poor track record when it
comes to anticipating the effects of change.

Every now and then, for example, you'll still see perfectly reasonable explanations of why microprocessors can't possibly get any
smaller or more powerful (contradicting Moore's Law), or why
networks are bound to get less efficient as they grow (contradicting Metcalfe's Law). This despite the fact that these "laws" offer the
best explanations we have for the dramatic increase in the pace and
scale of change.

Some of this, as we've seen, has to do with the impossibility of
predicting the *particulars* of the future. At the same time, however,
this uncertainty about change means that almost anyone can dis-
miss a particular change as wrong-headed or even impossible.

Look at the technologies I discussed a few chapters ago—computers, e-mails, instant messaging, and even cell phones. For years,
managers had to work hard to convince their accountants and IT
departments to allow these tools into the workplace. Not only

were they harder to cost-justify than office space or forklifts, but they were threatening—it was clear that they'd lead to disruptive changes in the way people behaved and the way a company did business. (Text messaging during a meeting is still frowned upon in most companies, but because it's a disruptive behavior, not a disruptive technology.) As that notable techno-savant and nineteenth-century British Prime Minister, Benjamin Disraeli, once said: "Change is as inexorable as time, yet nothing meets with more resistance."

Resistance to change is natural.

But, of course, you aren't really that concerned with whether Wilbur can fly or Moore's Law is still enforced. Nor should you be. You're more worried about the people on your staff who are complaining about the Caffeinator 3000. Not only is it too noisy, but the coffee it makes tastes "different."

People in your organization will resist change—we all do, to some extent. This is only natural. Considering how difficult and uncomfortable it can be, resistance (and grumbling and complaining) is inevitable. So you need to understand *why* and *how* people (including yourself) resist change, and what strategies you can use to lessen that resistance.

People tend to resist change even if it has the potential to be exciting, uplifting, and positive. Let me demonstrate this with a quick exercise. Think about an undeniably good change that's happened to you lately. For the purposes of my example, I'll look at the pros and cons of having children, although for those of you without kids, this could just as easily be about starting a new job, taking a vacation, buying a new house, or meeting the love of your life.

Having children is about the biggest change anyone can go through in life. You're creating a whole new person and watching him or her grow into an adult. What could be more exciting than that? But take a minute to make a list of all of the "pros"—the thrilling and exciting things that having and raising children has done for you.

Not so easy, is it? Most people can come up with a few plusses: the built-in joys that little babies bring with them, maybe some great family memories, or watching them grow up and turn into independent and hopefully responsible adults.

Now, for the "cons," make a list of what you *lost* when you had children. For most people, this list is a lot easier to put together: freedom, time, money, independence, privacy, vacations ... not to mention the hours of worry and teeth-gnashing that go with trying to be a good parent.

As you can see, coming up with the things that we *lose* in a change is much easier, even when the change is exciting and positive! But what about changes that *aren't* so great, the ones we don't have as much enthusiasm for?

For instance, someone walks up to you and says, "Oh, by the way, what you're doing is really great, but we're going to redesign your job." Naturally, you would get upset. One of the first things you might do is sit down and put together a list of everything you're going to have to give up; what it will cost you personally to make that change.

Your list might look like this:

I will have to learn new skills.

I will have to work longer hours.

I will have to move into another office (another building, another department, etc.).

I will have to report to another person (or, possibly, keep a whole different group of people happy!).

I'll have to go to more meetings.

I'll be responsible for a lot of things that I just don't feel that competent doing.

I'll have to give up coffee breaks with my friends in order to learn my new responsibilities.

Because you're not sure what the new job will *really* require, this "cons" list will be much easier to put together than the "pros" list. (Be honest, now: Did you ever even think of putting together a list of "pros"?)

No matter what kind of change it is—whether it's exciting, unexciting, eagerly accepted, unwelcome, or unwanted— our first and natural instincts are usually negative and resistant.

THE FOUR DYNAMICS OF CHANGE

The most important thing you should know about change is that every individual will experience four basic dynamics when dealing with it. These include:

1. A sense of loss
2. Ambiguity and uncertainty
3. Deterioration of trust
4. Withdrawal and self-preservation

Left to themselves, these four dynamics can feed on and react to each other, creating a sort of domino effect, which if not dealt with properly, can undermine your organization's efforts to change.

Here's an example of the first dynamic, a **sense of loss**:

"Congratulations, Mr. Employee, you are getting a raise *and* a promotion!"

"That's great, Ms. Boss, but it raises some questions in my mind: I'm not going to have to move, am I? My hours will be the same, won't they? My phone extension will stay the same, won't it?"

Needless to say, at least some of these expectations are bound to be wrong. Remember how easy it was to come up with negatives in the last example? The same is true when you first learn that things are going to change. Every aspect of your work situation suddenly becomes a little nearer and dearer to your heart—mostly because it's familiar and nonthreatening. And a list of things that you might lose in the change is remarkably easy to put together.

No matter how secure you may feel, the questions raised by your sense of loss inevitably lead to the second dynamic, **ambiguity and uncertainty**. Ambiguity and its first cousin, uncertainty, happen when you have more questions than anyone has answers, which is typical when a lot of change is going on. More often than not, your boss *won't* have answers to this kind of question—he'll be too busy trying to implement the change and may not have anticipated them.

These first two dynamics can lead to the third dynamic, the **deterioration of trust,** which can be one of the most difficult to work around. Say, for instance, your boss comes to you and tells you how one aspect of your job is about to change. He assures you that it'll be easy and that everything will be okay. Two weeks later, however, things are totally different than what your boss told you; your new responsibilities aren't easy; and it's not okay. What happens to your trust level? It goes down faster than the stock market after an increase in oil prices.

How does it affect your relationship with your boss? The next time you hear that a change is in the works, you might say to your boss, "It sounds like a good idea . . . but two months ago you said that last change was going to be easy, and it turned out to be extremely difficult. This time, before I commit myself, I am just going to have to wait and see how things go."

managing *DOWN*

HONESTY IS STILL THE BEST POLICY

Trust is still a powerful part of motivating your staff, but honesty or candor does have its limits in times of change. There will be things that you can tell them and things that you can't—for strategic, ethical, or legal reasons. A good general guideline is to be as honest as you can, and make sure that they know you'll share everything you can with them, as early as you can. If you have questions about legal issues or the limits on disclosure, talk to your own supervisor to get them straight before someone puts you on the spot.

In the Old Business Reality, the definition of *trustworthy* depended to a great degree on what I like to call the "shelf life of answers"—the longer things stayed the way you said they would be, the more I could trust you. Today, in the New Business Reality, that rule of thumb simply doesn't apply. Trust has to be built on something besides that dusty shelf full of old answers.

No longer is anything set in stone, or even sand. The best laid plan, structure, process, or system will change. And probably soon.

The same dynamic that changed your relationship with your boss will also complicate your communication with your staff and your colleagues. For instance, let's say you get information about a change that needs to be communicated throughout the company. You convey it to your colleagues, but within weeks, or even days, the information is no longer accurate. The result? Your colleagues' trust and confidence in you decreases.

Ah, but quick study that you are, the next time you get some important information, you take the opposite approach. Not wanting to misinform people again, you hold on to the information while you check out its accuracy. Meanwhile, your colleagues get it from another source. The result? Their trust and confidence in you decreases.

So the next time you get some information you do ... what? Your best bet is still to share everything you know. But working in an environment of rapid change means that you have to attach a strong and clear "disclaimer" to everything you say.

In the past "subject to change" was sufficient. Not anymore. Today it's impossible to overemphasize the likelihood of change when you pass along information: "This will change. I don't know how. I don't know when. But it will change." Also, be forthright about what you don't know. If you don't know, say: "I don't know."

For example: "I know last Monday I said *that* was the way we were going to do it. I know this Monday I said *this* was the way we are going to do it. I also recognize that the two are different. That doesn't mean you can't trust me or believe me. With what we knew last week, we were going to do it *that* way. With what we know this week, we are going to do it *this* way. The situation has changed, and we've changed to meet it. That has nothing to do with whether you can trust or believe me."

By saying "here's where things stand—for now" and reminding people that the only thing that's constant is change, you can slow down the deterioration of trust and short-circuit the rumor mill that can be so destructive to an organization.

Unfortunately, you're not always going to be able to maintain the level of trust you need. Sometimes you won't have enough information about a reorganization, or a new strategic direction, or a new accounting system, to make a reasonable judgment about where you stand and what you should do. Sometimes, in the midst of major change, no one will have the answers you need! And sometimes your colleagues just won't accept the information and reassurances that you offer them.

When an employee or an organization loses the sense of trust, a fourth dynamic, the **sense of self-preservation,** comes into play. For some individuals, self-preservation may take the form of passivity, inaction, and silence that they hope no one else notices. They may think to themselves: "I am not going to say anything, do anything, or contribute anything. It's just too difficult!" They are hoping that the change will just go away, and they'll be able to go on doing their job the way they've always done it in the past.

These people think that the best place to be in a time of change is "hunkered down, waiting for the storm to blow over"—not calling attention to themselves. They think: "If I stay below the radar, and management—or other arbiters of change—don't know who I am or what I'm doing, I can't be fired." Their motto: Stay in your office, don't speak up in meetings, and *never* answer your phone!

Ha! If it were that easy, everyone would be doing it. (Unfortunately, in many organizations I've worked with the majority of people are doing just that. How do you think *those* organizations are positioned for constant, complex change?) But any forward-thinking management team looks at every corner of its organization for people willing to step up and take accountability, raise their hands, and say, "Yes, I'll give this a try." The irony is that those who don't may actually stand out like sore thumbs. Your lack of participation only calls attention to the fact that you're not adapting to the change. And that is *truly* the riskiest place to be.

Other people resist more actively. They whine, complain, and vent their anger and frustration to anyone who will listen. "I can't do that! How much more are they going to ask of me? I don't need this anymore. . . . Those [insert the appropriate adjectives before the names of the change advocates here] are punishing us! Haven't they ever heard of the saying: 'If it ain't broke, don't fix it'?" What these employees are really hoping is that if they stir up enough trouble, their managers will have second thoughts about going ahead with the change—at least in their area.

THE ULTIMATE BAILOUT

Sometimes, however, employees offer the company an even more dramatic form of feedback—by leaving. This also boils down to self-preservation—good swimmers often jump ship first. That is, they may be dissatisfied *because* the company is *not* changing, *not* aligning itself to an ever-shifting world. They may be frustrated because they see the need for the modernization or the upgrade *even before the change has been announced or planned.* And when it doesn't happen on their timetable, they go somewhere where they think it might. They do this to protect themselves.

But not everybody leaves because a company isn't moving fast enough. Have you ever heard of an organization where everyone stays until they die or retire, whichever comes first? At any given moment, or for any particular reason, some people will leave any given organization. They may leave because they feel bored or frustrated or underutilized, and their feelings and judgments about their situation may be legitimate . . . or not.

There are actually two categories of these "bailouts": Those who quit and leave and those who quit and stay. It's the latter, quit-and-stay group who are the most difficult to work with—and these are also the ones who are most likely to hunker down!

Losing people is not necessarily a bad thing—if the people who leave are misaligned with the company's goals, changes, or new direction. It's worse if these employees stay, and say or do nothing, undermining the change. Eventually you'll need to track them down and help them get with the program . . . or help them decide to leave.

Ironically, those who do leave may turn out to be some of the greatest proponents of change—at their next job! Who most often asks, "Why do we do it this way?" Who usually has a wealth of new ideas to help improve a process? Who is usually the most willing to do whatever it takes? Who is eager to learn, to try new things? Who is ready and willing to start with a clean slate?

That's right! The answer is—drumroll here—a new hire. Where do new hires come from? Old jobs. The people so willing to do whatever it takes in a new job are often the same ones who were negative and resistant in their old job. In fact, many of them left the old job because they thought they couldn't do what was being asked of them. Or they didn't want to. Often the changes they regard as fresh and innovative at their new place of employment are the exact same ones that were "impossible" at the old place.

Fortunately, the difference between "I can't do it" and "I'll do whatever it takes" doesn't have to involve a change of address. All it really takes is a change of perspective.

Taken together, the overall effect of the four dynamics of change on your business can be like a toppling row of dominoes:

Sense of loss: "*This change could really present a problem.*"

Ambiguity and uncertainty: "*I can't get a straight answer about how this will affect me. I'm not sure even my boss knows the answers.*"

Deterioration of trust: "*I'm not sure my boss is telling me the truth.*"

Self preservation: "*First, I'm going to make sure that I've got my own job covered. I'm not going out on a limb for this organization.*"

Take a close look at these dynamics of change, and ask yourself: Do I see any of these reactions in myself—or others? The bottom line is that individual dynamics are inextricably linked to the progression in organizational dynamics: Stress and frustration go up; communication deteriorates; productivity takes a hit; you lose your momentum and commitment to change; people don't work as well together as they once did; there are power and turf struggles between departments; morale suffers; and you lose good people!

If this downward spiral sounds familiar to you, it's because you've probably experienced it before. But guess what? It's okay if you see or feel these reactions in yourself or in your fellow workers! Because these are the **natural dynamics of the change process.**

The point of this chapter is that it's okay to feel some resistance—and then move beyond it. Let me say that again—resistance, while counterproductive, is absolutely natural! And it's okay to resist change *at first.*

In the long term, though, these "natural reactions" can cripple your efforts to change, and do considerable damage both to your company's efforts to stay competitive, and to your career!

You need to overcome your resistance as quickly as you can. At the end of the day *you* have to be responsible for, and responsive to, the questions and situations raised by the changes. You have to start by accepting the limitations of what you and your organization can do to moderate individual reactions to change.

YOU WILL NEVER MAKE EVERYBODY HAPPY

So stop trying! There will be unhappy people no matter how you make a change. Change a lot or change a little. Change quickly or change slowly. Making everyone happy is impossible.

Besides, I believe happiness is a choice. Morale is a choice. Satisfaction is a choice.

If you keep trying to make the people you work with happy, then you are trying to solve the wrong problem. Only the individual truly controls happiness, morale, and satisfaction. Are you in business to make your employees happy—at the expense of your customers or profits, which control everyone's bottom line?

The fact is that many employees define satisfaction on the job as: "Leave me alone! Let me do my job the way I know how. If you keep poking and prodding me and asking me to do and learn different things . . . then I am dissatisfied!"

In the New Business Reality, you need to promote a new definition of job satisfaction:

I work for an organization that tries to adapt and align itself with the shifting and changing marketplace . . . and they challenge me personally and professionally because of it.

Even with this new definition, it's not going to be easy to provide employees with job satisfaction. But at least this definition accurately describes the risks and rewards of the world of work today.

Now that we've taken a look at some of the roots of resistance—and at some ideas that will hopefully help you move past them—let's try a slightly "updated" version of the pros and cons exercise you did earlier.

IS YOUR GLASS HALF FULL OR HALF EMPTY?

Let's see how you fare in your reaction to change. Let's imagine that you work at our example company, Forest Associates. Your boss has just broken the news that the entire computer system is going to be upgraded. Not only will this create the usual slowdown for several weeks, as your staff gets trained on the new system, but the new operating system has a reputation for being a little "buggy" and prone to crashing. However, once the kinks are worked out, the upgraded system should be much more powerful and easier to use, making your work both faster and more efficient. Now, make two lists of what you see as the positive and the negative effects of the change. Don't edit yourself; include whatever comes to mind.

Which list is longer? (I think we already know the answer to that one!) If a few of your immediate reactions were "I don't like the sound of this!" or "What was wrong with the old system?" don't worry, you are perfectly normal.

However, as we've discussed, if you and your co-workers can't get past this initial resistance, it can "domino" into a serious problem for Forest Associates. So let's add another step to this exercise with a little more detail for each entry. For each of the positive things you came up with, think of a corresponding action that would help you take advantage of it. For each of the negatives, think of an action that would help you minimize the problem.

For example, "This system is buggy" could be followed by, "Let's make sure that everyone using the system knows how to report the bugs they come across, so that our IT staff can get to work on them." "I've heard the system crashes a lot" could be followed by, "Let's set up a system of frequent backups so that we lose as little work as possible."

This step feels a little different, doesn't it? Instead of building on your natural resistance to change, you have taken your first steps toward moving past it. The problems you anticipated might still happen, but you are spending your time and energy on fixing those problems, rather than letting them get in the way of what eventually could turn out to be great progress for Forest Associates.

The next chapters will also help you redirect these natural reactions, by showing you how to communicate with your colleagues through the four basic phases of change. By understanding how change works its way through an organization, you'll find that you can spread the message of getting past resistance much more effectively.

SUMMING UP

- Resistance to change is natural. It's how you handle the resistance that makes the change successful.

- It's a lot easier to imagine the negative effects of change than the positive outcomes, even when the change is good.
- No matter what the change, each individual must face four basic dynamics: a sense of loss, ambiguity and uncertainty, deterioration of trust, and the need for self-preservation.
- These dynamics feed upon and reinforce each other, and if they are not properly dealt with, can result in a domino effect that greatly undermines the change and your employability.
- Change is inevitable and painful but the more effectively you deal with the organizational dynamics of change, the more likely you are to retain the workers who will best adapt to constant change.
- You can't make everyone happy; like satisfaction and morale, happiness is an individual choice.

05

THE FOUR STAGES
OF CHANGE

After reading through the last chapter, I imagine some of you are having second thoughts, saying, "Never mind! We didn't really need to reorganize our operations after all." I have to admit that just listening to the list of different "diagnoses" for how workers resist change is enough to give anyone a serious case of avoidance, not to mention a serious headache.

Maybe it would help if I offered a few more (mostly) reassuring thoughts here. First of all, remember the universal principle we discussed earlier: "We have met the enemy, and he is us."

Everyone, to some extent, experiences the different Dynamics that we've examined. Whether you're evaluating the performance of your direct reports, worrying about the reactions of your colleagues, or just looking in the mirror—knowing that these are natural *and* manageable issues can help you keep a level head during a chaotic period.

And the truth is—although maybe it's not as useful—that you're going to get some positive surprises as you learn to manage change. Maybe it's a system upgrade that goes so smoothly that you can toss out your worst-case scenarios; or maybe one of your "hunkered-down" employees suddenly "gets it" and becomes an unexpected champion for a new approach.

In Chapter 4, we talked about how resistance to change is part of human nature. As the rate of change increases, you can reasonably expect that people are going to demonstrate resistance more reliably and be less willing to participate in new initiatives without some serious reservations. So as you progress through your work career, it's going to be increasingly important that you learn as much as you can about managing constant, complex change. Employers and recruiters look at all kinds of skills, but in the future, the ability to work effectively in a changing environment is going to be at the top of their list.

With that in mind, you have to remember that we're discussing how people act. And people are complicated. People in groups are even more complicated. People in groups under pressure are maybe the most complicated of all.

So as much as I'd like tell you that this is a simple problem, it's not. You can find case studies analyzing companies in change that show all kinds of different behavior as being "typical" of the stressed, uncertain, untrusting, uncommunicative, and overly self-protective typical employee.

managing *UP*

KNOW YOUR LIMITS

Remember that results are everything and you have to do everything you can to produce them. But you're not likely to do your best work if you're stressed, sleepless, or confused about your role. And no one is going to thank you for work that's sloppy or full of mistakes. Find ways to get yourself back on track and back on task.

But it's also not your job to act as a therapist—fielding complaints, finding out what makes everyone "tick," trying to make sure that they're all happy at work. You cannot force people to give up their resistance to change, and you can't talk them through it. Your job is to identify problems and solve them—recognizing resistance when it starts, offering help and support where appropriate, and offering yourself as an example of someone who is successfully moving through the change process.

managing *DOWN*

KNOW THEIR LIMITS

There are limits to what you can expect from your employees. Reward employees who work hard, but if their work is deteriorating from stress, overwork, lack of sleep, etc., make sure to deal with the cause.

It can be a little daunting, even a little intimidating. Again, that's natural. Fortunately for us, the process of change and the problems that can arise are not as open-ended as they seem. Just like the four familiar aspects of resistance that we looked at in the last chapter, there are recognizable patterns of change that almost everyone and every situation shares.

For example, change *and* feelings of loss *and* resistance to change usually follow a regular series of events that we can look at as the **four stages of change.**

THE FOUR STAGES

As we've discussed, when organizations go through a change, most of the employees experience a sense of loss. Changes can include a merger, restructuring, downsizing, outsourcing, the installation of new technology, a shift in customer focus, or a new location, to mention a few. It doesn't matter whether the change is large or small, good or bad, it can still have a profound effect.

For example, consider a small group that has worked together for several years. Suddenly and without warning, most of their positions are eliminated as the company is downsized and the team disbanded. The lone surviving worker finds herself in a new department and location. Although in theory she should be thrilled to have survived the cutback, in reality she's apprehensive about having to deal with new responsibilities, a new set of personalities and a different departmental culture. Not to mention the guilt she may feel because her former coworkers are out of a job, while she is still employed.

The reaction to unwanted and unexpected change varies with each individual, but there are sure to be some consequences, no matter what. Even something as seemingly innocuous as working on a different account or working in a new location can result in a sense of loss: of routine, of workplace friendships, of a familiar commute, or even of places to eat lunch—all can have a powerful effect.

However, in most cases the response to change follows a familiar pattern. These phases or stages are similar to the "Five Stages of Grief" defined by the late Elizabeth Kubler-Ross in her book, *On Death and Dying*. Kubler-Ross studied typical stages—Denial, Anger, Bargaining, Depression, and Acceptance—that occurred in people responding to tragedies in their lives. Since then, they have been found to be a good model for just about every form of personal loss or change, from death to divorce to addiction—and even to positive events, such as a promotion.

Our stages will look a little different than Kubler-Ross's, to more accurately reflect how things work in a business environment. The four stages most people go through when confronted with change in the workplace are:

1. Betrayal
2. Denial
3. Identity Crisis
4. Search for Solutions

Understanding these four developmental phases will help you recognize problematic, yet predictable behaviors in yourself and others when faced with a change. Learning to recognize these behaviors should be a big advantage when the time comes to move beyond them.

Betrayal

A sense of **Betrayal** results from having something or someone that you need or depend on withdrawn without explanation. Causes of betrayal can range from losing a reliable supplier to losing an assistant, from having a star performer hired away by another company to a client switching to a new distributor. It can feel like you've just had the rug pulled out from under you! Reactions to betrayal vary from shock and disbelief to numbness and embarrassment.

Betrayal can take many forms and can mean different things to different people. During a recent seminar I invited participants from a very large company to give me an example of what they considered as a betrayal.

Much to my amazement, they started talking about frozen turkeys. Apparently these managers felt let down because they and their employees no longer received frozen turkeys for Christmas! Can you imagine the logistical nightmare of handing out ten thousand frozen Christmas turkeys? The only worse possible scenario would have been giving out live turkeys for employees to take home!

It didn't matter that the turkey was replaced with a gift certificate of equal and probably greater value. The managers felt betrayed because they didn't get their turkey. But the real kicker was that the switchover from turkeys to gift certificates had been made *twelve years ago*.

Every capital expenditure from that point on was compared to the lost turkeys:

"They can remodel the lobby . . . but they can't give us turkeys."

"They can upgrade the phone system . . . but they can't give us turkeys."

"They can put a new printer in every office . . . but they can't give us turkeys."

"They can buy TV ads during the Super Bowl . . . but they can't give us turkeys."

"They can send us to this seminar on change . . . but they still can't give us turkeys!"

Feeling and holding onto a sense of betrayal over something seemingly innocuous is hardly a unique phenomenon, however. When I asked another group about betrayal, someone mentioned the disappearance of the retirement party cheese ball. I wasn't sure I'd heard them correctly, I asked the person to repeat his answer and when he confirmed it, I posed the natural question, "Huh?"

It seems that for a long time, every retirement party at this company had featured a nice cheese ball. Suddenly, and for no apparent reason, the cheese balls were discontinued. The change could hardly have been a cost-cutting measure; we're not talking about a gold watch here. Nevertheless, the employees felt slighted.

Think about this for a moment . . . it's just a cheese ball, for crying out loud!

You really *can't* make up this stuff!

Now, in general I think it's a good practice to assume that people are not crazy. I don't think employees should assume their bosses are crazy, and I don't think bosses should assume their employees are crazy. And I'm pretty sure that the people complaining about turkeys and cheese balls are not crazy, either.

There are really two different dynamics at play here. The first is *betrayal.* The company took away a benefit, and for some reason it really stuck in the minds of this group that there was something fundamentally wrong and unfair about that action. So unfair that it has stuck in their minds for more than a decade, and so unfair that any number of genuine capital improvements—renovations, upgrades, investment in the business—pale by comparison.

That's where the second dynamic—*entitlement*—comes into play. I imagine that if you asked any of the employees, in advance, whether they'd trade the turkey or the cheese ball for a new printer, they would have made that deal in a second. So how did this become such a sore spot for them?

"Entitlement," taken literally, means that you have a right to something. For some reason, these employees had turned a gift from their organization into something that was theirs "by right." So, when the company stopped giving away the turkeys and serving cheese balls, they felt as if one of their rights had been violated.

This sense of entitlement can prove to be a major barrier to change in an organization. After all, while some employees feel entitled to foodstuffs, others may be attached to the same old way of doing things: the meeting they've always run, the sales call they've always made, the size of the bonus they've always received. This sense of entitlement can turn a legitimate change in business practices into something much worse—a betrayal.

The fact is that—in the absence of an employment contract—there is only one essential agreement between the employee and the employer: You work in the interest of the organization, and the organization will compensate you for that effort. Anything beyond that is a misguided sense of entitlement that can only get in the way of the change process.

Denial

Denial, the second stage, starts when you move beyond the initial shock into a state of disbelief. You can't, don't, and won't believe that the change is real. It's during this phase that you begin to suffer and start feeling anxiety and pain concerning the change. (The Betrayal stage is a little closer to Kubler-Ross's Anger stage.) You may think, "I don't know what this is going to look like nine months from now but all I know is, I don't like it." The change makes you uncomfortable, and you have trouble believing that you actually have to adjust to it. At this point, your main interest is to preserve the status quo.

Here's what denial can sound like at work:

"This isn't going to work."

"This doesn't apply to us because we are different/special/unique."

"This too shall pass."

"If you ask me, things will probably stay pretty much the same. They'll work through the crisis/not close the plant/let me keep my office."

"I will believe it when I see it."

"Even if it happens it won't affect me."

"Here we go again."

"It's the management 'program of the week.'"

"This will blow over. It always does."

"I've waited out four VPs and I can probably wait out one more."

"We tried this two years ago and it didn't work then. How can they possibly expect it to work now?"

And the old standby: "If I just keep quiet and do my job, I'm sure things will get back to normal soon."

If you find yourself or hear someone else saying something like this in reaction to the change, you can be pretty sure that they're still in denial.

Identity Crisis

The third stage is **Identity Crisis**. During this stage, people typically start out angry and move toward self-analysis. You can expect that you and your employees will begin expressing an emotional and occasionally dramatic response to the change. You may also develop a sense of withdrawal, lack of concentration, and alienation from the workplace.

It's typical for people in this stage to start asking two kinds of questions. The first kind expresses their anger at the change:

"Why should I do this?"

"I think they're trying to get rid of me."

"This really isn't what I signed on for."

"I've worked hard for this company for years, and all I get is this lousy reorganization?"

The second type of questioning demonstrates self-analysis, as employees try to figure out just where they fit into the workplace after the change is implemented:

"When will I fit in all this extra work?"

"Will I be able to adapt?"

"What am I going to do?"

"Will I have the resources and training needed to get through this?"

"Will I be able to handle the workload?"

"Is it worth it to come in and fight these battles?"

Which leads to the ultimate question, the elephant in the living room: *"Do I really want to be part of this organization any more?"*

Search for Solutions

The **Search for Solutions** is the fourth and final stage. It may take some time to get there—how long no one can predict exactly—but once you get there you will begin to see some gain or advantage from the change. Ordinarily, you won't get to this point until you've gone through the first three stages. And you may still feel overwhelmed:

"How am I going to get all of this done? Anybody got any ideas?"

"I need to figure out who is responsible for that these days"

"This new system has me confused. I've got to get some training!"

But as you and your colleagues begin to move into this stage, the comments will start sounding more positive:

"Let's do this thing."

"Let's get started."

"How about this? Here's an idea."

"This isn't as bad as I thought."

"Maybe we should we try this."

"That could work!"

This is also sometimes known as "seeing the light at the end of the tunnel." When you hear this kind of language from your staff, it means they're willing to give change a try, and accept that it's here to stay (at least for now). At this point, you should also see productivity start to rise again.

HOW THE STAGES INTERACT

The four phases of resistance can be directly tied to the drop in productivity we discussed earlier. Once we move into the **Betrayal** stage of change, productivity begins to drop off. People start to focus on the change and on their reactions—almost anything but the job at hand.

A recent study by the U.S. Department of Labor determined that the average productivity for a worker during an eight-hour day is 4.8 hours. During a transition or in times of change, productivity drops to 1.2 hours, a potential loss of 3.6 hours a day. Gossip and speculation escalate via water cooler gatherings, phone conversations, and even e-mail. Everything accelerates *except* for getting work done, despite the fact that getting it done has become even more important!

At some point after the changes have been announced, explained, and rolled out, employees will start to realize that yes indeed, this is the new "way things are supposed to work" from now on. When this message sinks in, most people move out of **Betrayal** and into **Denial**. They've accepted that the change exists, but they haven't accepted that it affects them. As you can imagine, productivity continues its spiral downward during this period.

The next phase is the **Identity Crisis**, which is often the most painful stage. Workers are uncertain and upset about their role with the company and can get very emotional as a result. And how do most organizations deal with emotion? They don't!

Either verbally or nonverbally, they tell their employees, "This is a job! If you've got problems, leave them at the door, will you? I don't want to hear about them, so get back to work!" Or they give employees the 800-number for corporate headquarters. Or they refer them to Human Resources or the company Employee Assistance Program (EAP) for short-term counseling.

The truth is that this is a good time to get emotional. It's normal and perfectly healthy to vent over what is an understandably upsetting situation. Whining, complaining, suffering, even some anger, should be perfectly acceptable. It's important to acknowledge your feelings because they are the impetus that will push you into the next part of this stage, *self-analysis*.

Productivity remains sharply down during this stage. After all, most of the company's energy is going into figuring out how the changed company will work. People often become self-centered, opinionated, know-it-all, moody, overly sensitive, and quick to anger during this stage. But they need to do this emotional "work" in order to get to the next stage, the **Search for Solutions**.

Here's a good example of this final stage from our friends at Forest Associates, who are still struggling with their new computer system. It is zippier and in some ways more efficient, but it does crash frequently, and some data has been lost. This has slowed down both their customer service and their ability to process orders.

managing *UP*

TECHNOLOGY THAT WORKS

Introducing new technology requires making decisions about where your company's and your customers' needs will be in the future. New systems take a lot of money and time to develop, and once they're started, they're difficult to stop. So if you're frustrated by the technology you have to work with, keep in mind that any technology is usually better than none. Discuss frustrations with your boss and your IT department, but make sure they know you're committed to making it work. Use your knowledge of work processes to contribute ways to fix the problem. And listen to your IT department. If they know you're willing to work with them, they may be able to help you.

The Forest Associates staff could have reacted in two different ways. They could have sat around and grumbled and complained about the new system, calling the manufacturer, calling their sales rep, hoping that someone would fix the problem for them.

Instead, they tried to figure out what caused the problem. Was there a pattern? A consistent occurrence that precipitated the crash? With a little detective work and some Internet research, they discovered that the software drivers for some of their printers were incompatible with the system. The system should work fine, however, with their newer printers.

So they simply disconnected the older printers—and presto! The crashes stopped. They accepted responsibility for making the overall change work and took the initiative for solving the specific problem they faced.

As already noted, the search for solutions is the point at which everyone's hard work starts to pay off. As more and more staff members reach this stage, you'll see productivity rebounding. You'll see it start to recover slowly, as more and more people begin working together in the same direction. Once this movement reaches critical mass, you will reach and hopefully surpass the level you started at.

RANGE OF REACTIONS

Everyone goes through all the four stages when faced with change, but different kinds of changes will affect different people in different ways. For instance, a small change in a routine procedure may only result in manageable spikes in denial and anger, whereas a realignment of the total workforce may cause a full-blown disruption in all four stages. In the worst cases, you'll face the Big Question of the self-analysis stage: *Do I really want to be part of this organization?*

Everyone goes through the stages at his or her own pace. For some people it takes a day; for others a week; and still others months. Some people never complete the stages and remain stuck in identity crisis or denial, despite your best efforts to help them. But the faster you recognize which phase you're in, the more quickly you can move on to the next one. And the better you are at recognizing what stage others are in, the more effective you'll be at helping them move themselves through the stage. And that's the key to getting the whole company through a particular change.

ARE YOU READY TO RUMBLE?

I don't want to give you the impression that it's okay for everyone to work through these stages at a comfortable pace. There are some very practical limits to how flexible you can be, and sometimes you're going to have to make people a little uncomfortable to encourage them to catch up with the rest of the group.

managing DOWN

DON'T LET THEM GET TOO COMFORTABLE

Judging how hard or fast to push employees is one of the hardest choices you'll have to make. Push them too hard, and you may increase their resistance. Don't push them enough and they won't take the need for change seriously. Many managers feel that "no news is good news"—that as long as there are no complaints, everyone is moving along at the right speed. Unfortunately, you're not going to hear complaints from people who have stopped moving! Your job is to get results, and that means you're going to have to pay more attention to how your staff is acting. Some managers keep careful notes of every interaction they have with their staff. Others can keep a rough tally in their heads of how each individual is performing. Find a method that works for you, but make sure your staff gets to where you need them to be.

First, you have to remember that the pace of change is increasing every day. If you're moving at a comfortable pace, you probably aren't moving fast enough.

Second, everyone in your company plays an important role (hopefully) in getting the company's business done. (If they aren't important, then why are they on staff?) If for one reason or another, half of your staff is still in denial about their role in the change, how can you or anyone in the company possibly take advantage of the new efficiencies and opportunities the change was designed to create?

For example, let's say that the boss at Forest Associates decides, "My customer service department needs to use the new computer system *right now* to speed up how quickly we process our customers' financial statements."

Some of the customer service employees may still be struggling with their feelings of betrayal and denial. They probably don't even want to think about processing the customers' statements. Hopefully, their managers can give them some extra time to work through their issues. But what if the competition is already expediting statements for their own customers? They're sure to try to lure clients away from Forest Associates by promising them the same treatment. The managers at Forest Associates can't afford to wait! They'll have to find a way to meet their customers' needs even though it means that some of their employees will be under extra pressure to move forward.

And so we need to work hard, and work together, to make sure that everyone in the organization completes all of the stages of change. At the same time, you still need to hold people individually accountable for moving *themselves* through the process. And to make sure that happens, moving yourself through the process must be a top priority!

WHERE ARE YOU?

This process has to start with you. Take a moment and think about the four stages of change. Now ask yourself: Where am I now? No matter what you do or where you work, I'm sure you are facing some sort of change. So sit down and take a moment to assess whether you're at the beginning of the process, dealing with your sense of betrayal, or toward the end and accepting and adapting to the new way of doing things.

In order to successfully deal with change, it's more important to understand where you need to go, than to know where you are. It's okay to be in betrayal and denial, but it's crucial that you know you need to move through all of these stages to complete the adjustment process. Just understanding your situation isn't a cure-all. Change is still difficult and painful! Yet as you experience change, and learn the best way for *you* to move from stage to stage, it will become easier.

Everyone is different, and everyone reacts differently to change. What works for someone else may not work for you. So experience and *practice* at dealing with change is invaluable if you want to become one of those rare individuals who can say that they're good at change. In this case, practice does make perfect!

CHALLENGING CHANGE

So far, in my effort to show you how change works in an organization, I've looked at change in a pretty uncritical way. But the New Business Reality is not about thinking that all change is good or that everything "before the change" was bad. There are good changes and bad changes, right changes and wrong changes.

managing *UP*

PLAYING FAVORITES

Change happens for all kinds of different reasons in an organization. Changes made because of office politics, personal relationships, laziness, etc., do not serve the customer or the organization. This kind of change is worth talking to your supervisor about. Just make sure you understand the purpose of the change before you complain. And make sure that you can explain any resulting problems and have suggestions for fixing them. It's more important to come up with good solutions than to point out problems.

I think you'll find that most people don't need your help when it comes to challenging change. It's easy to sit in the break room gossiping about the missteps that are an inevitable part of every change process. Or to send e-mails ridiculing the new way of doing things. Anyone can say: "That's a dumb idea. What will those idiots think of next?"

It's much harder to know when you have a legitimate reason to challenge a change that's already in the works. Once started, change develops its own momentum, and it's better not to try to stop it unless you can show how the change will hurt the company and its customers. Focusing on the customers and how the change will affect your relationship with them makes it much easier to know when to challenge, and when to accept a change.

It's better to try to modify the change from within the change itself. By getting involved, you can take advantage of its momentum to help "steer" the process in a more productive direction.

What needs to be adjusted? What should be rethought? If an aspect of the change isn't working properly, how can you fix it and make it better? It is okay to challenge a change if you realize that you may need to come up with a workable solution.

Chapter 6 will discuss different ways to communicate so you can deal effectively with the stages.

SUMMING UP

- When confronted with change in the workplace, most people go through four stages: betrayal, denial, identity crisis, and search for solutions.
- The stages of change are directly tied to a drop in productivity, so you need to move through them quickly.
- It's acceptable to experience strong emotions during a change, but you must work through them to avoid getting stuck.

- Working within the change itself is the most productive way of dealing with it.
- You are accountable for getting yourself to the Searching for Solutions stage as quickly as possible.
- Using the customer as a barometer will help you more accurately judge the value of change.

06

COMMUNICATING THROUGH THE FOUR STAGES

WHAT *NOT* TO SAY

In the Old Business Reality, communication about change usually followed a simple formula, something along the lines of: "We'll do it my way because I said so—and I'm the boss!" If it works, the results can be a beautiful thing—no questions, no complaints, no foot-dragging, and no ambivalence.

The problem is that things hardly ever work that way in the New Business Reality. Today, your success at creating change depends heavily on your ability to communicate the change to the people, branch offices, vendors, departments, and consultants you work with. Some of these people may not even work for your company. Certainly, not all of them have to "jump" when the boss says "jump." Some of them may actually resent being told to "jump"— and by communicating ineffectively, you risk losing some of your most important allies.

Instead of starting to get a sense of why the change is necessary, your employees and colleagues may withdraw to the betrayal stage, not unlike those in the previous chapter who have been "talking turkey" for the past dozen years!

Unfortunately, many business leaders and managers haven't learned how to communicate effectively in this new business environment. Their management experience may be based in the old "command" reality, or they may be under pressure to get results, waiting for the timing and conditions to be perfect, or simply pressed for time. And sometimes, the way things are said doesn't seem as important to them as what needs to be said.

In the New Business Reality, it is often more important just to get issues, changes, and problems out on the table, rather than waiting until the timing or the conditions are perfect. Because "perfect" never happens, does it? Likewise, the *method* of communication is often equally important as *what's being communicated*. This communication is likely more involved than what's been communicated in the past, so it NEEDS to be as effective and targeted as possible.

managing DOWN

THE PURSUIT OF PERFECTION

As the French pundit Voltaire put it, "The perfect is the enemy of the good." Sometime the pursuit of perfection is an excuse for avoiding difficult jobs or not producing. This is especially true in communication—it's much more important to stay in touch than to say exactly the right thing at the right time.

But if you want to learn to be effective as a change agent or leader in your business, you have to develop a new and different approach to communicating about change.

In the previous chapter, we looked at how people at the *same* company, experiencing the *same* change, can be in different stages of the change process at the same time. As it turns out, each of these stages requires a specific kind of communication; a customized "way of saying things."

These different kinds of communication are tailored to the specific needs and questions people have when they're at particular stages. So, first, we'll look at three basic types of communication and how each is suited to the different stages. Your goal will be to learn to communicate in a way that helps move others through to the next stage of change.

THREE TYPES OF COMMUNICATION

The first, **Informative Communication,** contains the basic information that people need to do their job—who, what, where, when, why, and how—stated clearly. It can take the form of announcements, agendas, plans, schedules, team meetings, presentations, etc.—anything that gives associates new information about their work. Informative communication should also include the business case for the change—explaining why it's necessary and how it will benefit the customer, and, therefore, the organization.

The second, **Supportive Communication,** is exactly what it sounds like. It includes the communication equivalents of hand-holding, counseling, sympathy, and empathy. This form of communication has an emotional component and requires more sensitivity and patience. Many managers have trouble adapting to this type of communication. Unfortunately, it is also one of the most important parts of the effort to get workers to commit to the change process and move on to the next stage of change.

The third type, **Inspirational Communication,** is what you're probably used to hearing in company meetings about change. This is the rah-rah, the-future-is-bright kind of talk that managers use to build enthusiasm, team spirit, and to motivate people for the change. In the right place, this kind of speech can be very powerful, but if it's used at the wrong time it can actually set back your efforts at change.

What to Say and When to Say It

As we've discussed, everyone goes through the same four stages of change, and our friends at Forest Associates are no exception. Richard Greene (not his real name) manages a support staff of twelve whose jobs are being redesigned now that the new sales accounting system is in place. He thinks that all of his staff has gotten beyond the **Betrayal** stage, and he's tentatively identified eight who are still in the **Denial** stage, along with four who have moved on to the **Identity Crisis** stage.

In the morning, when he first comes in, he sees the "denial crew" busily working at their desks but doing things in the old and outdated way. As he heads toward his office, he can hear the other four whining and complaining.

From what we've learned so far, it should be clear that Richard can't respond to all of his staff in the same way. He has to "customize" his message to fit their specific needs and concerns. How should Richard communicate to these two groups?

managing *DOWN*

ONE SIZE DOESN'T FIT ALL

The days of one-size-fits-all management are over. It's no longer enough to stand up in front of your department to outline the shape of things to come—you won't reach enough people that way to be effective. Managers in the Old Business Reality could count on the "because I said so" method. Today's organizations and employees are different, and a command approach just won't get it done. No one said it was going to be easy, did they?

Since the majority of his staff is in the **Denial** group, let's look at how Richard should deal with that group first.

The key to talking to people in both of the two initial stages—**Betrayal** and **Denial**—is to use **Informative Communication** At this point in the change process, people are questioning the whole idea of the change and trying to understand how it will (or won't) affect them. People in these stages appreciate communication grounded in hard facts and business realities.

He may have to answer questions like these:

"Why?"

"Who says so?"

"How long is this going to last?"

Any question that includes the word "me" usually falls into this category, for example:

"What does this mean to me?"

"How will you measure me?"

"What do you expect of me?"

"How will you compensate me?"

He should always focus on making the business case, the "why we are doing this," making the connection between the change and the customers and marketplace clear.

If, instead, his employees hear only encouragement or cheerleading at this point, they may suspect that there really aren't many facts or a business case to support the changes. And then they're highly unlikely to back his efforts to create change. The sooner he can get them to understand what he's looking for, recognize why it's important to Forest Associates, and how it affects their work (and more importantly, the customer's), the sooner they will be able to move out of these two stages.

managing UP

"KNOW THYSELF"

This ancient Greek maxim applies in the workplace as much as any place in contemporary life. It's especially critical when your organization is going through changes. You need a good basic sense of who you are and where you are in the process of change to move forward.

The rest of Richard's employees have the factual information they need, accept the situation, and have moved on to trying to sort out what they should do about it. They are in the next phase, the **Identity Crisis**. Much like adolescents (or adults in mid-life crises!) people in this stage aren't sure of their role in the reconstituted organization, and they will need a lot of his time, attention, and **Supportive Communication**. He will need to be as patient as time allows and show them that he understands what they're going through. He might say things like:

"Look, I know that you've worked at Forest for a long time, and this must be hard for you."

"I really understand what you're going through. It must feel like your first day at Forest all over again."

"What skills do you think you'll need for your new responsibilities?"

"I want to help all I can . . . but it's really up to you to move ahead."

When Richard gets into his office, the four employees who are in **Identity Crisis** immediately pester him with questions: "What about this?" and "What about that?" "What about me? "How am I going to fit in?" "Here's what I don't like about this." "It just doesn't seem like the Forest Way of doing things," and so on.

People in identity-crisis mode can be tough to deal with. They're whining, complaining, and carry all kinds of negative emotions. Like most managers, Richard will find them an unwelcome drain on his time and energy. He may think, "Why can't these folks just go away and leave me alone? At least the other eight are quiet and not making waves." Richard may be tempted to reprimand or even discipline the four—just to put a stop to the questions.

managing DOWN

THE SUNNY SIDE OF THE CUBICLE

As a manager, keeping a positive attitude in the office can be one of your biggest challenges. After all, you probably understand the problems more than anyone else. But showing a negative response or attitude can reduce the effectiveness of your entire work area. Any difficult situation requires a little self-control over your response. But in a changing organization your "audience" is extremely sensitive to the signals you send out, so your "acting" must be especially convincing.

But the truth is, it's counterproductive to punish people for having an identity crisis. Keep in mind that everyone has to go through all stages before they can create solutions for the customer. Does he want to keep the workers in denial? Yes, it might be easier in the short run for Richard to tell the four in identity crisis to act more like the rest of the team, because he's tired of their questions and complaints. But he runs the very real and serious risk of those four employees moving *backwards* in the process, returning to the

Denial stage themselves. If he punishes or otherwise squelches them, they *will* go straight to their coworkers—and maybe even start to adopt their "hunkered down" approach to the problem.

They'll tell their co-workers things like: "Hey, you were right . . . Forest Associates doesn't care about us anymore. I'm just going to sit here like you until this all blows over." And although the people in denial have their heads down, they are watching. They'll reinforce their own message, saying: "I told you not to go into Richard's office and ask that question." He could end up with *twelve* people who will sit there month after month as though the change had never happened.

As Casey Stengel once said: "The key to being a good manager is to keep the people who hate you away from the people who are still undecided."

managing *DOWN*

YOUR WORK ISN'T ALWAYS YOUR JOB

Sometimes, being a manager means making hard decisions that affect the lives of the people who work for you. Wouldn't you rather escape into your office and exercise your prerogatives to do a little, uh, real work? Keep in mind that the times when your actions have the greatest effect on your staff are those when you need to be most present and most attentive, so that you can tell whether your actions have gotten good results.

Richard's only choice, and your only choice, is to be as patient as he can, answer as many questions and objections as he can, and encourage his employees—in a firm but supportive way—to move on to the next stage. He cannot make the change for them, or even force them to go through with it. Richard should make sure that his employees know that while the organization appreciates what they're going through, they're responsible for moving *themselves* through the changes quickly. It's also his job to make sure they understand the urgency of the process—that the rest of Forest Associates can't wait for them! And that their ability and willingness to move through the process now becomes part of performance.

Hopefully, Richard's staff will begin to see the light sooner rather than later and move on to the fourth and final stage of change, the **Search for Solutions.** Now is the time for **Inspirational Communication,** which has been the stock-in-trade of change consultants and management experts operating in the Old Business Reality.

Now and only now, after people have accepted and begun to adapt to the change, are they really ready to listen to the rah-rah. And even then the inspirational communication needs to focus on good business practices and common sense. At this point, Richard might say:

> *"Boy, it's amazing how much faster our customers will get their invoices, isn't it?"*

> *"We're really going to be able to take some business away from Meadows Consulting."*

> *"This positions us to be much more competitive going forward."*

> *"This reduces the maintenance costs of the old system dramatically."*

His goal is to keep reinforcing his messages about what he needs them to do, and why it's good for them—and Forest Associates— to do it.

MISCOMMUNICATION AT WORK

Let's take a quick look back at what we know about the change process to see if we can figure out why companies going through changes experience so many—and such severe—communication problems.

We've already looked at the fact that it doesn't matter where you are in the organization—just about everyone experiences the same four-stage transition! Whether you're in upper management or an entry-level worker, you'll have the same basic emotional response to change.

Now let's look at a second fact that we've discussed and think about how the two facts work together in an organization. As mentioned earlier, senior-level managers usually go through the four phases before the rest of the company. It's sort of a trickle-down effect: those who design and start a change will (obviously) know about the change first. Upper management will be the next to know, then middle management, supervisors, and then employees. Those who know about the changes first (and especially those who helped design the change program) have more time to adjust to it—more time to work through the four stages. So in the typical company, each level of management is likely to be at a slightly different point in working through the four stages than the levels above or below them. Higher levels will be further along; lower levels will be lagging behind.

There's an important aspect of this that should be considered. We've seen that different styles of communication are appropriate for the different stages of change.

However, most of us communicate in the style that fits the stage that *we're* at, not the style that fits the person we're talking to.

Each level goes through the stages of change at different times. As a result, at any given point in time there are going to be major gaps between the different groups—both in terms of their progress *and* in the kind of communication they're likely to use, and need.

Typically, by the time a company announces a major change, the vice presidents will have made great progress toward the end of the change process. They'll be at the **Search for Solutions** stage and therefore gung-ho to pump up their staff with inspirational, go-get-'em talk. At the same point, employees, who may have just found out about the changes, are still reeling with the shock of **Betrayal** or in **Denial**. They'll be looking for more substantive and **Informative Communication**.

You can imagine what happens. (Many of you have probably seen it in action yourself!) At the first meeting announcing the change, a senior manager will get up and start spouting to the employees: "This is going to be *great*! We're going to re-matrix our advancement options and reposition ourselves in the marketplace. There will be great opportunities for everybody!"

In the meantime, the employees, who haven't had nearly as much time to adjust, are probably and understandably in shock. As far as they're concerned, the manager has just dropped a verbal bombshell, yet he acts like he's expecting applause. They're not hearing anything substantive, so they really have no idea how it affects *them*. How can they tell whether it's a pipe dream or something worse? Worse yet, it involves *change*, and who knows whether that—whatever it is—will work?

So these employees will see their senior level managers as out of touch, unrealistic, and uncaring. They may feel the managers have no idea of what they need to do their jobs, nor do they appreciate how hard they, the employees, already work. They may make an immediate transition, not toward the change the company is looking for, but into a state of **Betrayal**. "We used to be such a family around here. Look at all the problems that these changes are going to create. The management obviously doesn't care about us as much as they used to."

On the other hand, senior-level managers may regard employees as ungrateful whiners and complainers with a bad attitude. They won't understand why the workers don't respond to their enthusiasm and "leadership." How can they fail to see how important and productive the change will be? And why they don't even seem to be listening to what they, the managers, are trying to say?

managing *DOWN*

THE LIFE CYCLE OF A RUMOR

At first, when just the vice presidents are involved, information filters its way down through the ranks as warnings and rumors. No one knows or will admit to knowing what's going on. During the next step, after some kind of formal announcement is made, employees try to read the points like tea leaves, searching for hidden plans or secret agendas, second guessing everything that's been announced, and speculating about what hasn't been. In the third step, the announcement becomes a cause for general criticism of the company and its management.

This may sound harsh but it's fairly typical of companies that do not deliberately manage how information about change is communicated. Notice that each of the three steps emphasizes negative communication. This is why it's so important to understand the natural gap in communication that occurs during times of change.

GETTING IN SYNC

These gaps explain where the problem in communication comes from. They create the cynicism and the skepticism, the distrust and the suspicion between management and staff. The only way to close the gaps is to understand where you are in the phase process, know what type of communication you need, and make sure you get it.

Even more important, you need to understand where others are in the stages of change—and give them the kind of communication they need!

Here's a great example of this process: I was giving a seminar a few years ago and noticed that everyone at the front table was whispering intently among themselves. It seemed like my talk about communicating at different levels had struck a chord. The table, which consisted of the communications department of a large company, had spent the last several days crafting an internal e-mail memo about a huge organizational change that was going to be sent out to ten thousand employees the following morning. The first line of the announcement read, "Great news! We're changing everything."

Imagine ten thousand employees reading that. Click . . . Delete! No one would get past the second line. At best, ten thousand employees would be sent spiraling down into a sense of betrayal and denial. You can probably imagine the effect on productivity that cheerful little announcement would have.

So the group at this table went back and rewrote the announcement memo, using the following suggestions:

1. The first paragraph contained **Informative Communication.** They explained the situation to their employees: "This is what we are doing and why. Here is how it will make an impact on our customers and service. This is how it will affect you and what we need from you. We will measure the success of the change by doing A, B, and C."

2. The second paragraph contained **Supportive Communication.** They said: "We know that this will be difficult for

many of you. We will help—and here's how. We'll have an employee meeting every Monday from 8:00–9:00 A.M. Every Wednesday we'll set up "skip level" meetings so you can talk directly to upper-level management. You can also post questions to a special page on the company website at any time—and someone will respond within twenty-four hours. Also, any workers whose jobs are directly affected by the change will get additional training. Here is what you will get and here is how you will receive it."

3. The third paragraph contained **Inspirational Communication**, including an explanation of how the change was going to help the organization and the rewards everyone would reap after the change was effectively in place.

Note that this announcement included all three kinds of communication in an effort to cover everyone in the company, at any stage of change. This is typical of a broad, mass announcement. As you can imagine, if this memo had been aimed at a group of new employees, or a group of senior managers, if would have been more focused on their specific needs.

Of course, the communications department had started with the best of intentions. Most people do. But if it were possible to move an organization through the process of change with only inspirational communication, there wouldn't be nearly as many problems as we see in the real world, nor would you need this book! I wish I could just send you an e-mail saying, "Trust me, this is going to be great. You'll love it. It's downhill, it's sunny, it's effective, and it's golden. Just two months ago I was where you are today. I know that writing with your off-hand looks dumb. But look at me . . . today, I'm ambidextrous!" But that wouldn't be true. Change is often painful, and change in organizations can be extremely frustrating. You job is to learn how to not only make that process manageable but turn it into a competitive advantage.

Like death and taxes, it's unavoidable, but you can make it easier for yourself and everyone you work with.

THE RULE OF REPETITION

There is one more simple rule of communication that I'd like to share with you: the Rule of Repetition. While it sounds like a card game that you'd play with your kids, it really means that you have to tell someone something multiple times before you can be sure that they've heard your message and they believe you. That's right. Not once or twice, but several times!

managing DOWN

THE PROPER USE OF THE RULE OF REPETITION

Whatever you do, don't say, "If I've told you once, I've told you ten times not to do X, Y, or Z." Not only does it sound condescending, which can build resentment, but it's a good way to turn the rule of repetition into the rule of infinite and *ineffective* repetition.

So in the New Business Reality it's not enough to get up in front of a group of people and tell them that change is here to stay, that it won't be easy, and that they're accountable for making it work. (I think that makes twice....) The concept of change is such a difficult one, and people are so good at resisting it, that you need to reinforce it continuously and consistently. People need to hear your message from different directions, in different modes and mediums, in staff and department meetings, in individual discussions, in e-mails and on the company website, and any other method you can use to communicate with your employees.

You also need to continuously and consistently address the symptoms of change—the depth and duration of the drop in productivity, and the kinds of resistance and stages of acceptance. It may seem extreme, but to make change work you need to become the "change channel," constantly broadcasting your company's message of change.

managing *UP*

PROPER RESPONSES TO THE RULE OF REPETITION

Whatever you do, don't start finishing your boss's sentences once he's reminded you three or four times not to do X, Y, or Z. Not only is it impertinent, but he also may lose count of how many times he's told you and start all over again.

A few final notes about the Rule of Repetition

First, getting the process of change right is like aiming at a moving target. Everyone will have different reactions; everyone will go through the four stages at their own pace; and everyone needs communication in a form that they can process. You will need to constantly evaluate and adjust what is and is not working and redesign your message to fit the new "facts on the ground."

Second, and this is really a hard truth to face, if you happen to say or do something that is contrary to what you've been telling others, you will have to work extra hard to regain their trust in your communication. In other words, if you're not consistent, the Rule of Repetition can turn into the Rule of 99 or the Rule of 999. Now you have an issue of credibility, and you'll have to work even harder to prove yourself.

SUMMING UP

- You must learn how to communicate effectively in dealing with and adapting to change.

- Three different types of communication—informative, supportive, and inspirational—are appropriate for the different phases of change.
- Pay close attention to the questions people ask, as they provide valuable clues about which phase they're in and what type of communication they require.
- Change has a trickle-down effect: managers hear about it first and go through the phases much earlier than front-line employees, and the type of communication you use must reflect this.
- Follow the Rule of Repetition—which says you need to tell people something multiple times before you can count on it registering with them. Be consistent and unrelenting in your communications.

07

BUILDING A CHANGE-ADAPTIVE CULTURE

So far we've been looking at change from a close-up and personal perspective. We've looked at a range of different individual behaviors, reactions, and communication styles in an effort to understand how change works in an organization.

But if you really want to get your organization solidly on the path to success in this New Business Reality, you also need to take a step back and look at it from a broader, organization-wide perspective. After all, we're really interested in where "the rubber meets the road." You need to understand what happens when all of these individual dynamics come together in the workplace—with dozens if not hundreds of people working together and sharing their experiences of change, for better or worse, with their own individual fears, insecurities, and styles brought together in one effort.

I know, sometimes it's hard to understand how *any* work gets done in the workplace environment, much less how any change happens! Asking for coordinated and effective change seems to be setting the bar pretty high!

And it is. But that's where we are today. The increasing demands made on you by information, communication, and customers mean that it's not okay just to keep doing things the way you've always done them. Not only do you have to raise the bar on your expectations for yourself, but you also have to figure out how to raise the bar on the performance of your entire organization.

After all, while you may have to manage individuals, and these individual perspectives will come in handy in that context, no one's going to thank you for developing a few enthusiastic advocates for change in your area if your department as a whole isn't pulling its weight in the company-wide change initiative.

So while the first part of the book concerned itself with the local effects of change on individuals, and what to do about it, this part is going to be about change in the organization. It doesn't matter how good you are at change if you're the only person who's changing.

Developing an organization-wide perspective on how change works and what you can do to accelerate it is absolutely crucial, because this is where an organization can gain a large part of its competitive advantage in today's chaotic and ever-changing business environment.

This is one of the central ideas of my thinking about change. In today's marketplace, an organization gains competitive advantage by getting to be good at change—by creating a truly "change adaptive" culture that can adjust quickly, efficiently, and effectively.

Let's be absolutely clear about this. Creating a change-adaptive culture is very different from changing the culture. "Changing the culture" implies a single event in response to a single problem—changing the culture from plan A to plan B.

But we've already seen that this is a luxury we no longer have in the changing marketplace. Probably, you never again will face something as simple as a single change with a discrete starting point and finish line.

If only it were as simple as getting the desks moved, the phones changed, and everyone in their new jobs with their new assignments. Once again, change is much easier if you can see the light at the end of the tunnel and know that someday soon the change will be over, and you can start to get acclimated to your new status quo.

managing DOWN

PREDICTING THE FUTURE

Consistently getting good results requires you to get a little bit ahead of your customers. In many cases they don't know what they'll need two or three years down the road—even if that's how long it will take you to develop a solution that meets their needs. Know your industry, the competitive environment, and especially new developments in the field, and keep an eye on what your customers will need in the future.

But as we've discussed, the reality of the situation is much more difficult. Not only do you face disruptive change in the workplace, but you also face overlapping waves of changes—many, many changes at once, pushing and pulling you in all directions, with little or no hope of ever reaching a new equilibrium.

Even before you finish one change, you have to turn to take care of a whole series of new changes. In essence, the end result of change is a moving target, even when you're able to draw some direction from your customers:

"Is this available in green?"

"Everyone's telling us to be a little more daring. Purple seems to be growing in popularity."

Again, change comes in like a series of waves—or maybe thunderstorms! If your customers tell you they'd buy more of your product if it were only green or purple, you can't ignore them and insist that you're only going to offer it in brown or black. But, again, you can only predict the future in general, not in particular. After you and your staff have spent tons of time and energy producing new designs in new colors, you may find that your customers have already moved on.

"Do you have anything with stripes?"

"I think I liked that old brown better."

Even if you are able to "perfect" a company culture that supports and adapts to change, don't think that your work is done. Once you understand change and its demands, and how to organize your business around it, you'll realize that being able to change means that in many ways your work is just beginning.

However, there are also real—and dramatic—benefits. Once you've "gotten good" at change, you'll also be able to take advantage of a whole world of new business opportunities that you could only dream of while you were stuck in the Old Business Reality. And with customers and markets changing faster and faster every day, you have to get better at change just to stay within shouting distance of your goals.

WHAT DOES A CHANGE-ADAPTIVE CULTURE LOOK LIKE?

I have spent a lot of time with organizations helping them transform themselves from traditional businesses into new change-adaptive cultures. Generally speaking, they come to me for advice because in certain respects they're already "sold" on the concept of change. People certainly don't look me up if they want to avoid change!

Their first step is pretty predictable. They ask me what they need to do to change their organization into something new and change-adaptive. "Here we are—an organization that wants to be changed!" They usually don't know the half of it.

"Should we get on the Internet?"

"Should we adopt an open office plan?"

"Should we fire all the vice presidents?"

Guess what. This is still the old organization talking—and it doesn't really want to be changed! Or maybe more accurately, it wants to be just "a little bit" changed—instead of transformed into a truly competitive, change-adaptive culture. You cannot use the old culture to create the new change-adaptive culture. You cannot use the old approaches, thinking, or behaviors to suddenly create new approaches, thinking, and behaviors. You need to attack the old culture from a completely new, different, and unexpected direction.

As soon as members of the organization listen to my change-adaptive message, they understand that in some ways they've opened a major can of worms (or maybe, but not to give away the rest of the chapter, they've opened up a major barrel of monkeys!) What they thought would be merely tactical turns into something a lot more challenging:

"Great, you moved over here, like I asked. But I really meant over there."

"What would you do if I told you that purple has just been named the color of the year?"

"I know you just got comfortable in that chair, but I think I need to sell it to the highest bidder."

The difference is subtle, but the difference is also HUGE. You don't just need to change your company's culture, you need to change it so that it stays changed and keeps changing. You need to replace your traditional methods of setting and implementing your goals with one that is directed from outside the company—by that constantly shifting, changing, moving target called: the marketplace!

That is what I mean when I say: You need to develop a change-adaptive culture!

Not everyone agrees with me on this, but I believe that your efforts at change, and the decisions you make about what you're going to do and how you're going to apply your resources, should be directed at a single target—serving the needs of your marketplace and, especially, your customers.

Now, I understand that sometimes it's difficult to identify "the customer" and that in some businesses you have lively debates over who this customer actually is. Some businesses, for example, sell only to brokers or wholesalers. Are their customers the brokers? Or the end consumers?

Let's say you're in health care. Is your customer the patient? Or is it the insurance company that pays the bills?

To me this is something of a distinction without a difference. It may be more difficult to track your customers if you're not selling to them directly, but the end customer is still the customer who matters. In most businesses, brokers and wholesalers try their hardest to follow the customer—and if they can't sell it to the end customer, they're not going to buy it from you!

You'll have to make the final judgment about who your customer is—who you're trying to serve. Make it carefully and thoughtfully, because you're going to build your entire business plan, and your new change initiative, around that choice. However, what I do suggest is that whomever you define as your real customer lies *outside* your walls. There are no internal customers when it comes to aligning the organization.

managing *UP*

KNOW YOUR COMPANY CULTURE

Before you stop paying attention to quantitative measures or due dates and start paying more attention to your customers' needs, make sure your boss is aligned with this new measure of success. In some companies making the sale, closing the deal, reaching targets, etc., is the *only* thing that matters. You can still redefine what success means to you as long as you keep these organizational goals in mind. They should all ultimately tie to the final customer.

MONKEY BUSINESS

At the beginning of this book I promised you a story about monkeys. Monkeys are great fun, aren't they? They're smart, clever, curious, and can be great troublemakers. I'm sure you've all seen the TV commercials with monkeys wearing ties, sitting around a conference table, making important decisions about the future of the company. Stories about monkeys also offer a great opportunity to point out some of the excesses of office behavior—without having to name names.

But this story is a little more serious—it's about how monkeys learn and especially about how monkeys learn in groups. Which is very relevant to our discussion about change and how it takes place in organizations.

You may be familiar with this specific story, known as "The Hundredth Monkey," because it's very popular with people interested in social and cultural change. It's based on a real anthropological study done some years ago, but the point isn't so much in the scientific details as in the general pattern of behavior that the story reveals.

In any case, a few years ago a group of scientists decided to research the roots of societal change. They designed a field experiment in which they'd introduce a new kind of food to a controlled population of monkeys, to see what they did with it and how long it took for the group to include the new food in their diet.

They chose an isolated island populated with only about 300 monkeys. They left a supply of potatoes on the beach and then sat back to see how the monkeys would react. It wasn't long before a few of the monkeys came down to the beach and started playing with the potatoes. Monkeys are naturally curious, so more and more of them came down to the beach to see what the fuss was all about. Eventually, one of them just had to know whether these new objects were edible—he picked one up and took a bite out of it.

Well, as you can imagine, the monkeys discovered that the potatoes were GREAT to eat, and the majority of the monkeys on the island spent the rest of the day at the beach, playing with and eating the potatoes.

The next day, the scientists came back and dumped another pile of potatoes on the beach. This time the monkeys were ready. It only took an hour or so before nearly all of them were at the beach. On the third day, the monkeys were *waiting* for the scientists to show up. So far, they had shown a pretty good ability to learn the food value of potatoes.

But what happened next was even more interesting. As part of the scramble for potatoes on the third day, one of the monkeys accidentally dropped a potato into the island's lagoon. Afraid that she'd just thrown away her lunch, she reached into the water, pulled it out, and took a quick bite.

To her surprise, she learned that potatoes dipped into the lagoon—where a lot of the dirt and grime got washed off—tasted even better! And from then on, that monkey would wash her potatoes before eating them.

Now how do you think the other monkeys responded? You would think that they'd all start washing their potatoes. Monkey see, monkey do, right?

Well, it turns out that monkey behavior is a little more complicated than that. Instead of copying the potato washing, the other monkeys' first response was to isolate and ostracize this innovator. What the potato-washing monkey had discovered seemed suspiciously *different* to the others! None of the monkeys had ever washed any of their food before, and this change in eating habits seemed *unconventional* and therefore somehow *wrong*.

As time went on, however, more and more of the island's monkeys began to discover how much better the washed potatoes tasted, and they began to wash their potatoes too. As the number of "innovative" monkeys began to grow, the reaction of the "traditionalists" grew harsher, even violent.

The larger group of "traditional" monkeys would go down to the beach, form a circle around the pile of potatoes, and eat until they'd had their fill—shutting out the minority group of "innovators." Then, while the potato-washing monkeys ate what was left, members of the larger group would throw rocks at them, call them names ("spud dipper" being one of their favorites), and generally harass them!

Slowly but surely, though, the number of potato-washing monkeys grew larger and larger until one day the 101st monkey dipped a potato into the lagoon, washed off all the dirt and grime, took a bite, and discovered that it really did taste much better.

At that point in time, on that island, monkey society reached a critical turning point. The following day, what do you imagine all of the other monkeys did? Yes! As if it were the most natural thing in the world, every single one of the remaining monkeys began to wash their potatoes. "Spud dipping" had become the new status quo! No apologies, of course. No regrets offered for their past behavior.

This little story of "monkey business" has always been one of my favorites because it offers a nearly perfect example of the way behaviors change when large organizations go through major disruptions.

As we've seen in the previous chapters, different people have different reactions to the stresses and strains of change. As it turns out, their behaviors fall into three general categories: there are those who go along willingly, those who need a little nudge (well, maybe more than a nudge), and those who have to be dragged kicking and screaming the whole way.

There are some very clear similarities between these three general types and the behaviors shown on Monkey Island. All of the monkeys on the island were involved in a cultural change and can be categorized into one of our three groups. There were the early washers, the wait-and-see'ers, and the angry mob of nonwashers.

I like to define these as *design, default,* or *defiant* behaviors. Let's take a closer look at each of the three types so that we have a better idea of what these behaviors might look like when we finally get back into a human organization:

Design monkeys are those who started washing their potatoes as soon as they saw another monkey doing it. As far as monkeys go, these are on the leading edge, the pathfinders, the trailblazers. What do you think it takes to be a design monkey? What are their common character traits? Curiosity. Self-confidence. Open-mindedness. Being willing to try something different and new. Courage. Guts. Being able to stand their ground in the face of strong opposition. Thick-skinned. Being able to take the rocks, the criticism, the abuse. What about conviction? What about the belief that they had discovered a better way? What about tenacity or perseverance or just simple stick-to-it-iveness? What about leadership and individuality? In other words, design monkeys are characterized by a lot of very positive and powerful characteristics. But they have definitely chosen the road less travelled.

Default monkeys are the ones sitting on the fence. They are the undecided voters of the monkey world. They'll wait to see how things work out between the designer monkeys and the defiant monkeys, but they are by nature conservative in terms of change. You may hear them say, "I've never washed my food in my entire life. And look how well I've turned out. What a dumb idea!"

What are they waiting for? They're waiting to see what happens. Waiting to see if there are consequences for the designer monkeys. Waiting to see how many monkeys try potato washing. Waiting to see which side ends up in the majority. Which way the wind is blowing. What everyone else ends up doing.

They're asking each other:

"What do you think?"

"What are you going to do?"

If potato washing becomes the new norm, and everybody starts washing their potatoes, this group will be quick to join the "winning" side. "I sure am glad that I've been washing my potatoes since the beginning. This is the best thing since the microwaveable banana."

Or, if potato washing never catches on, if it turns out to be just another passing fad, well, that's okay, too. "I don't think anyone is washing their potatoes anymore. Sure am glad I never experimented with that. What a dumb idea!"

The **defiant** monkeys are the ones throwing the rocks, calling names, hoarding the potatoes, leading the charge against the potato-washers. They simply can't understand why anyone would wash a potato, or any food for that matter. Food is meant to be eaten quickly, before it's lost, stolen, or runs away. They refuse to try potato washing, because they're sure they're right. After all, monkeys have been eating food the same way for generations. And they're willing to be aggressive about their resistance, because they realize they're protecting something: the status quo, the way things have always been done, the culinary traditions of their ancestors. They are protecting themselves from having to change—from the risk they run by doing something unfamiliar and possibly dangerous.

I don't think I really need to give you examples of what defiant monkeys sound like. You've probably heard it at least once in every meeting you've ever attended. And on every day that you've been in the office.

"Who does she think she is?"

"Well, that's really going to screw things up for the rest of us."

"Has anybody tested the long-term effects of potato washing on monkey digestion?"

"Ewwww! Dolphins have been swimming in that water!"

Now, just for the sake of relevance, let's take a look at how these behaviors operate in a human context.

DESIGN BEHAVIOR

What do you think design behaviors look and sound like in your workplace? As they demonstrate design behavior, people will say:

"How can we make this process better?"

"How can we simplify it?"

"How can we make it easier?"

"What would happen if we just stopped doing X?"

Another sure giveaway is that the most common word out of a designer's mouth is "customer." Customer this and customer that. What do we need to do to serve the customer better? The second most common word is "why?"

"Why do we do it this way?"

"Why can't we try it another way?"

"Why does everyone have to wait so long?"

Before we go further, please note the following:

I'm using the word "designer" to describe the role an innovator, a risk taker, a changer, someone who EXHIBITS DESIGN BEHAVIORS. If you're really a "designer" in the graphic arts sense, you may also be a designer, but you have to fit the profile!

What are some other characteristics of design behaviors in the human workplace? Here are a few suggestions: Showing initiative, taking risks, rocking the boat. People who fall into this category are always ready to go. They tend to be impatient. They're always onto something new. They also tend to step on toes and make some of their colleagues a little bit uncomfortable. As a result, they are sometimes called names, not invited to meetings, and are the last to hear about the doughnuts in the break room. (Sound familiar?) They can be criticized for speaking up, criticized for making suggestions, and criticized for doing their job too well.

"For Pete's sake, why did you have to go and do that? Now we're all going to have to show up at meetings ready to X, Y, and/or Z."

What does design behavior look like around the office? You can almost always identify people who exhibit design behaviors by their level of participation. They are actively involved in the work process—both in terms of getting work done and making suggestions about *how* the work is done. Whether this person is in the minority or majority, whether her boss agrees with her, whether or not she gets her way is not material. Even people who challenge you, question you, and argue with you are exhibiting design behaviors *if* (and I know that can sometimes be a pretty *big* if . . .) they are participating in your business and their intent is in alignment with your customers and the marketplace.

These are your staff members who sit where they can participate in meetings, take notes, talk about meetings after meetings, clearly thinking about the discussions and the decisions that have been made. Even if they don't participate, if they're thinking about how to use what they've learned in the meeting, then they're exhibiting design behavior. If as you read this you've been thinking about how you can use the information in this section to help your business and especially your customers—then you fall into that camp, too!

A quick distinction here: Wondering about how the meeting applies to you is *not* design behavior; thinking about how you'll use the information when you go back to your desk *is*.

And there are other, slightly more sophisticated ways to look at design behavior. Holding a meeting or setting up a working group to study a problem or identify customer needs is only the most basic kind of design behavior. Expert "designers," the kind you hope to encourage in your organization, are more likely to skip the analysis stage and move directly to action. They are not going to wait for a meeting to kick around different ideas about how to change. They would rather just fix the problem, rather just make the change. You'll find them asking for forgiveness rather than waiting for permission, to quote the old adage.

If you're a manager, this may take some getting used to. "You know, boss? I just saw what needed to happen and did it. I didn't have a chance to call you. I hope you don't mind."

If they're truly exhibiting design behaviors, you have nothing to worry about. You'll be able to count on their sense of alignment with your customers' needs to make the right decisions.

managing *UP*

DON'T SURPRISE ME!

One of the best ways to keep your boss happy is to never surprise her. If you're not sure how much latitude you have in decision-making, try to clarify it with your boss by asking about specific limits in advance. Don't ask general questions like "Can I approve any expense under $100?" That's going to get tangled up in corporate rules and regulations. Do ask about specific existing decisions: "Were you comfortable with the way I handled X"?" or "Would it have been okay if I made that decision about discount on my own?

DEFAULT BEHAVIOR

What do you think default behavior looks like? Again, default behavior is pretty easy to identify when you listen to employees talk about change. You'll hear things like:

"Let's wait and see."

"Let's not get ahead of ourselves."

"Sounds like a great idea, but . . ."

"I'm not sure how that applies to my department."

"Plus ca change, plus c'est la meme chose." (Just in case you don't read French, that's "The more things change, the more they stay the same.")

Two key words that you'll hear from default speakers: "But . . ." and "Whatever . . ."

"We'll do whatever you decide."

"We'll do whatever we're told."

Or, most depressingly, just: "Whatever . . ."

One of the biggest problems with default behavior is the potential for a major disconnect between what people say and what they actually do. And it's what they end up doing that really counts. For example: "Looks great! Let's do it. I love it." *Time passes.* Then, spoken in quiet voice to self: "Thank goodness that doesn't apply to me."

Default behavior in the workplace uses almost every excuse and method of avoidance or delay that you can think of:

"Sounds like a winner but I don't think I'm the right person for that."

"I don't want to get involved in that part of the business."

"Let me know how that works out for you."

"Are you sure we have the resources for that?"

"That's not in my budget!"

"We're really too busy to take something like this on right now."

"Have all the vice presidents signed off on this?"

"Maybe with a little more research we'd know if this would work."

"Can we bring in my cousin, the consultant, to weigh in on this?"

"Let's set up a pilot program in your department."

And the always popular: "That's not my job (department, responsibility, area, etc.)."

Some of these may turn out to be good advice, but they are all being offered in an effort to slow down—if not stop—change. To make it seem too difficult, too confusing, too risky. To tie it into other organizational issues that will slow progress to a crawl.

Sometimes default responses attempt to stop change before it gets started:

"The board will never go for that."

"The regulatory panel will never go for that."

"The vice presidents will never go for that."

Maybe they're right, maybe they're wrong. Some people will go along, and some won't. But calling in these big negatives before you've gotten started is default behavior for sure. If, however, someone says, "Our customers will never go for that," you are hearing design behavior, which is always worth checking into.

Delaying tactics are also popular:

"I'll change my behavior when everybody else changes theirs."

"Just wait six months. We'll see if any of this stuff is still around."

There's also a strong element of self-preservation in default behavior. I once did a session for a client, and one of the company's senior vice presidents was sitting in the back, watching his twenty-five direct reports. No matter what I did that day, the only response I could get was essentially that of the SVP. Every time I asked a question, heads swiveled to see what he was going to do or say. And then I'd get a "yes" or "no" or rolling of eyes—nearly in unison.

The truth is that most people are so threatened by change that they'll go to great lengths to convince themselves that default behavior is okay. Imagine the following interior monologue:

"I hope that someone else will answer that question. I hope somebody else is going to participate. I hope somebody else decides to bring up the real problem. Me? I'm just going to see if I can make it through the meeting without getting into trouble. Don't want to risk the questions. Don't want to risk the *assignment!* If they can't see me, they can't ask my opinion. I'll just hide back here behind the vice presidents. If anybody looks over here, I'm sure one of those guys will answer."

Sound familiar? I hope not too familiar! But I'm sure we've all heard it before at one point or another. This is a good example of trying to protect the status quo—your own status quo.

managing *DOWN*

PREACHING TO THE QUIET

Believe me, just because you get the silent treatment in response to your questions doesn't mean you're facing a default or defiant audience. Sometimes people are tired, threatened, or just don't know the answer. Try not to encourage phony enthusiasm. If your message isn't getting the kind of response you want, go back to the drawing board and redesign the way you're presenting it. Either way, raise the bar on the level of expected participation. They need to tell you what they are thinking and why they may not be participating.

And, as you'll see later in this chapter, there's much more default behavior in the typical workplace than anything else. Different people can put different values on it for different organizations, but sometimes it seems as if 90 percent of what goes on in a typical organization is default behavior. (I guess it's clear why this is called "default," right?) In gambling, this is known as playing with a stacked deck. The odds against you are long, which is why it's so important to learn how to work around default behavior.

DEFIANT BEHAVIOR

Finally, the most dramatic form of resistance to change: defiant behavior. What do you think this looks like in an organization?

Compared to default behavior, the responses you'll get from defiant behavior are usually clear, unambiguous, and hostile to the very idea of change:

"I'm just not going to do that . . . and you can't make me."

"You know how much trouble it's going to be to replace all of the people who will quit, or you'll have to fire, if you do that?"

"You adopt that new tracking system, and I'll quit."

"I'm filing a grievance with the union."

"You're trying to destroy this company."

"We've been doing it our way for twenty (thirty, forty, fifty, etc.) years and we're still in business."

And the ever popular: "That's not in my job description."

Sometimes people don't even have to speak to let you know that they're defiant. It can be a hostile glance, a groan, even a nervous shifting in chairs. You can see it in their body language: arms crossed, frown on their face, leaning way back in a chair and rolling their eyes to the ceiling. The message is just the same:

"Can you believe he said that?"

"This is a complete waste of my time!"

"We could have saved a lot of time and money by just not having this meeting."

"If you think I'm opening up about the real problems here you're crazy."

My brother worked for a courier service while he was in college. He found out posthaste (maybe that's a poor word choice) that you just don't do a four-hour delivery route in four hours. If he did his job the way he was expected to, he'd immediately hear about it from the defiant workers in the organization:

"Don't make me look bad. I can get paid for six hours to do that route."

"If you do want to get done early, just go park the truck somewhere else and bring it back when it's time."

And, believe it or not: "You're setting an awful example for the rest of us. Now management will try to make all of us work harder."

This kind of behavior is extremely difficult, and in some cases impossible, to overcome. These employees don't care about the customer, they only care about protecting the comfortable work life that they've been able to carve out for themselves. And, for one reason or another, they feel they have the rights and the leverage so that they don't have to change.

managing UP

LITERARY RESISTANCE

A classic example of defiant behavior is the character in Herman Melville's *Bartleby the Scrivener*, who responds to every request from his employer with, "I would prefer not to." Bartleby's character refuses to accept change—even when his employer moves away—and eventually dies because he "prefers not to" eat. Melville wrote the story in the 1850s, but the message about defiance still rings true today.

DEFIANT BEHAVIOR AND DESIGN BEHAVIOR

Sometimes it's difficult to tell the difference between design and defiant behavior. It's not as simple as identifying the people who cooperate as designers, and the uncooperative ones as defiant.

Managers who have to execute a change strategy *love* people who cooperate. It's not easy to get a lot of people to change their direction, or their traditional way of doing things, and the cooperators at least *seem* to make a manager's job a little easier.

However, when you study change in organizations—where it's really worked and really delivered a tangible payoff—you find that that's not always true. Sometimes the best cooperators turn out to be the biggest drag on the organization's performance. And sometimes the most difficult people are the ones who make sure that the change actually works.

The best advice I can give you for evaluating behavior is to look at the things people say and especially do and judge them not in terms of cooperation but in terms of alignment with the customer. True design behaviors are *always* directed at this alignment.

The question of whether people are defiant or designers boils down to whose needs they focus on. If they focus on their customer's needs, then they're designers. If they focus on their needs, or their employee's needs, or their department's needs, or even management's needs (when they don't match the customer's), then they are defiant.

I'm sure you've worked with people who seem angry, obstructive, or even destructive. They're never happy. Nothing you do is ever good enough. They've always got something to add, they always think they know a better way; they're always rocking the boat, pushing back. They don't understand the need for consensus, or even the need to be civil to colleagues with whom they disagree.

managing *DOWN*

WAKING UP ON THE WRONG SIDE OF THE DESK

Of course, just because someone is cranky doesn't mean that they're exhibiting design behavior. Stress or lack of sleep can lead to the same "symptoms." Again, make sure you have a pragmatic view of an individual's contributions—which are more important than their temperament on any given day.

On the other hand, how people demonstrate their design behaviors does count. All the old business reality rules of respect and communication and tact still apply. Just because you demonstrate design behavior doesn't mean you can be a @#$% about it.

These are often not the most pleasant people to work with. They may be, however, some of your best designers. In fact, if they've been trying to push you, your team, your department, your organization closer to alignment with the needs of your customers, then you've got to try to ignore their abrasive side and accept the message that they're trying to send, in their own idiosyncratic way.

Just because they are loud, obnoxious, a pain in the rear to work with . . . doesn't mean that they are defiant. It boils down to what they are protecting.

You have to be careful not to confuse defiant behaviors with anger, unhappiness, stridency, emotion, or disagreement. Remember, just because I disagree with you doesn't mean I'm defiant. Even more importantly, remember that just because *you* disagree with someone in your organization doesn't mean that you're defiant, either. Keep our basic definitions in mind:

Design: Focus on the customer.

Defiant: Focus on the status quo.

Here's another way of looking at it. Ask yourself the following question: Do you need defiant behaviors in your organization? The answer is a conclusive *no.* You don't need or want defiant behaviors in your organization. If you find them, your job is to root them out, because defiant behaviors will hurt your efforts at change.

Now ask yourself a similar question:

Do you need people in your organization who disagree, who push back, who question the organization? The answer is a conclusive *yes*; you do need them. If their input is aimed at the best interests of your customer, they are a great example of design behavior.

You don't want people who go along with everything you suggest without question. You don't want people who go along to get along. You want people who can ask good questions and make good suggestions that help you increase your organization's alignment with the customer. If they're doing it in the interest of your customer, that's design. If they're doing it just to stall, to confuse, to try to short circuit the process of change, that's defiant.

managing *DOWN*

LEARNING TO LISTEN

Unfortunately, people who think they have a great idea don't want to wait to be heard. Expect them to bring up their ideas when it's least convenient, and expect them to bring along some direct criticism of your ideas, just in case. One great idea can turn a company around, and capturing that idea is the most important thing. So let your idea people sound off. It won't always be a happy conversation, but be able to evaluate all of the ideas your staff comes up with.

Let me offer another example from our friends at Forest Associates. Ashley runs a small marketing group that creates communication materials for the company. Let's say that one morning Ashley walks into their workspace and announces: "I have great news ... great news! We've decided to streamline our approval process for marketing pieces. Instead of the fourteen signatures you need now, you're only going to need twelve."

Alfred, the one person in your group who is never happy, always crabby, always complaining, is sitting in the back of the room. He raises his hand.

"That's a dumb idea!"

Patiently, hopefully, Ashley asks, "Al, why do you think this is such a bad idea?"

"Well, instead of twelve signatures, we only really need two. Mr. Pine and Mrs. Elm are the only two people who have ever asked for any changes to those materials in the whole time I've been here. If they're the only ones who sign off on it, we can get the materials out to our customers that much faster."

That, my friends, is what design behavior sounds like. Even though it requires a more radical change to the process, and some thinking on the part of the other twelve "approvers" about whether they really have a good reason to be on the distribution list, Alfred's suggestion is genuinely aligned with the needs of the customer—and that's the kind of change Ashley wants to encourage.

managing UP

EMPLOYEES ARE MEANT TO BE HEARD

As in all social situations, you have to use your common sense in deciding when and how to make your suggestions or criticisms known. Many companies place a premium on workplace calm and consensus building, and you may need to tread delicately to get your message across. Still, it's your responsibility to share what you know.

Now that someone's broken the ice, a few others in the group are ready to contribute. One is Andy, the department's assistant manager, who has been with Forest Associates since the dawn of time and knows more about this part of the business than almost anyone else.

He sticks his hand up in the air and says:

"Based on my experience here, I don't think either of those suggestions is going to work."

Patiently and respectfully, Ashley asks him, "Why not?"

"Well, there are a lot of reasons. First of all, these are pretty important materials, and everyone needs to make sure that we keep our quality up. Second, it's hard to know which of the fourteen of us will catch something wrong—we all notice different things. Third, there's room for fourteen signatures on the current form. So maybe we'd have to pay to have new forms printed, not to mention that we'd have to revise the manual, which says we need all fourteen signatures. And fourth, we've gotten really efficient at circulating things like this quickly—I can't believe that we'd save that much time. Finally, we've always done it this way at Forest Associates. We're really good at keeping everyone involved."

All pretty plausible reasons, right? And maybe Andy's arguments add up to a pretty convincing case for just leaving things alone.

Still, of course, this is defiant behavior. Its primary goal is keeping things the same in the marketing department—not on aligning the process with the customer's needs.

Ashley has some explaining to do. She's going to have to make it clear that the goal is to speed up the process for the customer, *not* to make things easier. At this point, she's responsible for communicating the business case for the change.

managing UP

LISTEN CAREFULLY

Simple stories, otherwise known as "ancient history," can be an invaluable learning tool in an organization. How many times have you heard, in learning or training situations, something along the lines of "Don't make the mistake Mr. Firr made. It took us years to recover those files." Case studies like these not only help you understand the process but also the urgency or risk behind it. Also understand that things are different today, and the reasons that something did or did not work years—or even months—ago may be different as well.

EVEN MORE CONFUSING

Even trying to preserve the status quo can be a design behavior. How? When your status quo is already aligned with the needs of your customers.

The New Business Reality does not require change for change's sake. Believe me, you're going to find plenty of things that need changing. And remember that every one of them will reduce your productivity. The truth is that you're probably already doing plenty of things right—that make the best use of your resources and that align with the needs of your customers. The last thing you want to do is change one of those *out* of alignment! Sometimes it makes just as much sense to leave things the way they are.

Keeping unnecessary change out of your workplace is just as much a design behavior as anything else you do.

Your definition of design is not *change* ... your definition of design should be *aligned.* That sometimes means change, but sometimes it means *don't* change.

It even requires you to *resist* change—if it isn't in the best interests of your customer.

THE MIX

Now that we have a few key definitions in place, let's take a look at how this mix of behaviors functions in the workplace.

First of all, whether you agree with it or not, you are involved in change in your organization in one of these three ways. No exceptions! Wherever you work and whatever role you play in your organization, it needs to keep changing to thrive in the New Business Reality.

Let's use a pictorial depiction to help us understand this situation better. First, draw a large circle. Let's pretend that this circle is really a pie chart that shows your daily work-related behaviors. Now, split it up into pie-slice-shaped sections to indicate what percentage of your workday is given over to design, default, or defiant behaviors.

This is another key idea. Design, default, and defiant are *behaviors*. We not talking about people or types of people. No one person is purely design, or purely default, or purely defiant. We all demonstrate *all* of these behaviors at one point or another during a typical day.

So, what percentage of your day-to-day work life are you typically spending in design, default, and defiant behaviors? You may not have thought about your workday this way before. It is possible to exhibit design behavior in a meeting about a reorganization but default or even defiant behavior when it comes to the budgeting process. And this is okay. On any given day, sometimes I'm design, sometimes I'm default, and sometimes I'm defiant, too.

Most people, especially those committed to change in the workplace, are surprised to find that the more time they spend thinking about and categorizing their daily experience, the more of their time ends up *outside* the design wedge. If this happens to you, it doesn't mean that you're a drag on your company—in most cases, it just means that you're forming more and more accurate assessments of your own work behavior.

The real question here is whether you can identify these behaviors in yourself and then determine which of them predominates in your behavior in the workplace. If you end up with 100 percent of your time spent in the design area, I'd have to say that I think you're fooling yourself. (Because you're not fooling me!)

If you really want to have your eyes opened, trying asking a few of your colleagues to give you their honest opinion about how much time you spend in each of these areas. Have *them* draw a pie chart that shows your typical day.

Then, when you're willing to talk to them again, make sure to thank them for the feedback. Remember that your ability to influence change in your organization depends to a large extent on how others see your behavior. So this is really invaluable information about the image that you're projecting. It almost doesn't matter how accurate it is, or whether it matches your self-assessment. Knowing how your behavior looks to the outside world can only help you be more effective and influential in the change process.

There's another reason that this is a good exercise, and that's because it's an excellent introduction to design behavior. Not only does it engage and involve you in a process that will lead to better alignment with your clients and customers, but it also gives you a great benchmark for where you are and where you need to go to be an agent for change in your organization.

Now let's draw another circle and mark it up with the profile for your entire company. Base this on your assessment of the mix of predominant behaviors in your organization—how many of your colleagues are predominantly design, how many are predominantly default, and how many are predominantly defiant?

Developing your own personal profile for these behaviors is important, but whether your organization succeeds or not is going to depend on what this overall profile looks like. In my experience, most organizations end up with a breakdown like this: 20 percent of the group is involved by design, about 60 percent is involved by default, and the remaining 20 percent is best characterized as defiant. Of course, the numbers for your group may be different, but this is fairly typical of organizations in transition.

Now, I am going to give you the benefit of the doubt. Just due to the fact that you're motivated enough to read this far, you've shown enough commitment to the change process that I'm going to count you as one of the 20 percent who behave by design. Congratulations! This makes you a thought leader *and* an agent of change! But before you let this go to your head, think about where this puts you relative to the rest of your organization.

Right! It means that the other 80 percent of your organization is watching you. Just like the design monkeys, you have now joined a minority of individuals who have targets on their backs. Why are the others watching? They want to know what will happen to you as a consequence of your advocacy for change. They want to see whether you're harassed or rewarded for your role in innovation. I'm sure you remember the old adage, "You can always tell the pioneers by the arrows in their backs!"

Now are you feeling a little less comfortable? Fortunately, one of the positive characteristics of your design "profile" is that you're probably not passive. You're active, engaged, involved—and you're certainly not going to just wait around for the sky to fall, are you?

Of course not! And, in the next chapter we'll look at a few key strategies you can use to make sure that your company ends up transformed into a change-adaptive organization—and you end up with the rewards you deserve.

SUMMING UP

- Organizations in the New Business Reality gain a large part of their competitive advantage by becoming good at change.
- Just changing your company's culture isn't enough—you need to transform your organization into a change-adaptive culture.

- Individuals dealing with organizational change demonstrate three different kinds of behavior: design, default, and defiant. Design behavior is the key to effective change.
- Every person and organization displays a mixture of these three kinds of behavior. The task is to encourage design behaviors.

08

THREE KEYS TO
MANAGING CHANGE

By now you should be something of an expert at recognizing how people respond to change in the workplace. But that's not going to help you influence the "enemies" of change—or even the "passive resistance." As I've said many times throughout this book, you can't force people to change—you can only provide them with opportunities to change themselves.

At the same time, you're at least partly responsible for change in your organization, and you will be judged in terms of just how successful you've been in bringing it about. Nothing is more frustrating than to be able to identify these kinds of behavioral issues without knowing what to do about them. Whether it's your own feelings of betrayal or crisis, or a department full of defiant employees who won't even listen to your explanations, you've got to find a way to execute your change strategy.

And soon! Your boss isn't going to wait, and neither are your customers. You can't afford to wait! Otherwise you're going to be left behind with all of the other struggling organizations that couldn't keep up with the ever-changing marketplace.

THREE PRINCIPLES FOR MANAGING CHANGE

So how do you influence those you need to influence, change those you need to change? As it turns out, the recipe for fostering organizational change is fairly simple and involves applying some of the lessons we learned from our island full of monkeys.

The basic problem is how to be effective—how to encourage change in a workplace environment—where both your influence and your resources are limited. The answer is surprisingly simple, although getting the details right can be tricky. You need to implement three basic steps to get the situation back under control:

1. Demonstrate design behavior.
2. Reward design behavior in others.
3. Create a critical mass of design behaviors.

I work with organizations and culture change—especially in transforming companies into more change-adaptive cultures. In all of my work, from day-long seminars to year-long consultancies, I've found that being effective boils down to these three basic principles. Let's look at these three steps one at a time.

First, **Demonstrate Design Behavior**. I think this one is pretty obvious. A lot of people call this "walking the walk."

One of the major problems with change is that newcomers to the process sometimes have a lot of trouble imagining just what the change is going to be like, and how it's going to affect them. So instead of adopting change, no matter how promising it might sound (remember this from earlier in the book?), they tend to be pretty conservative in their actions.

Until, that is, they see some examples of people demonstrating design behavior in the workplace—and seeing that they get rewarded for it, and not criticized or ostracized. In this case, your job is to be a living, breathing example of how people will work and interact with each other as the changes are made. That way, fence-sitters and other will see that it's okay to be involved with the change—it's not really as risky as it might have seemed.

managing *UP*

NO SENSE AT ALL

You may wonder why so many aspects of changes you've heard about don't make sense to you. The purposes of some features of a change may not be obvious at first. Pay special attention to the parts that don't make sense, and ask for explanation or clarification. In most cases the parts you don't understand are critical to the overall process. In some ways, if it feels "right" at the beginning, it can't represent a significant change.

Remember the Rule of Repetition! If you don't demonstrate design behavior on your own, the task of getting people to listen to your case for change becomes much more difficult—the rule of 99s, or the rule of 999s.

Second, **Reward Design Behavior in Others**. You're probably already familiar with how and why this works, especially if you have kids or pets. The goal is to get more of the behavior you reward. Pets, kids, co-workers, managers, supervisors—you can talk to them until you're blue in the face about how important change is to your organization. Some people get lucky with their pets. Some people get lucky with their kids, at least until they're in their teens. In the workplace, the "talking cure" isn't as reliable as you need it to be. Maybe you'll convince a few people. Maybe a few of those will even give your change a try. But that's a big "if" to bet your success on, right? On the other hand, if you reward design and design-compatible behaviors—you will almost certainly get more design behaviors, and as a direct result you'll get more positive change for the customer.

managing *DOWN*

TOKENS OF APPRECIATION

Rewards don't have to be M&Ms, or movie tickets, or extra time off. Because you're trying to influence the behavior of a group of people, rewards that are public and involve recognition, thanks, better assignments, or more influence work best. You want to reward the design behavior, but it's more important to spread the message throughout the company about how to earn these rewards.

Third, **Reach Critical Mass.** Reaching critical mass is the most powerful tool you have.

What is critical mass? It isn't a large group of people willing to criticize your work. (Although in practice it may sometimes seem that way.)

And it doesn't mean that a lot of people will get together and try to change things by pure force of numbers. Although people sometimes try, as is shown in the following example of a small telephone sales team at Forest Associates.

"Someone needs to talk to the boss," Tim Woodley said to his co-workers. "There's no way our customers are going to give us the information we've been told to ask for."

"I think you're right, Tim," said Anne, who sat in the next cubicle. "If we all tell him together, he's sure to see things our way."

"You're the best salesperson, Anne. Would you go with the rest of us to talk to him?"

Unfortunately, by the time Anne got to her boss's office, her colleagues had lost both their enthusiasm and their willingness to back her up.

"Mr. Chestnutt? We all got together and figured out that this new policy can't possibly work."

Mr. Chestnutt responded:

"What do you mean, we?"

That's when Anne noticed that she was the only other person in Mr. Chestnutt's office.

Anne was lucky, though. Mr. Chestnutt also wasn't sure how customers were going to respond to the new questions. It was important to him that they not offend Forest's customers, and he wanted to hear what kind of response the sales team was getting. Anne promised to let him know. Mr. Chestnutt promised to keep Anne's "change initiative" just between the two of them.

Critical mass is the 101st monkey. It's the point when enough people in your organization understand and support the change that most of the rest of the company goes along willingly.

Critical mass does represent the force of numbers, but not as a brute force. It's the point where the payoff for the change becomes so obvious that more and more people start cooperating, and you see a sudden, dramatic movement in your direction.

In the same way that all of the monkeys on the island finally started washing their potatoes, everyone in the organization will finally just "get it." They will participate, advocate, make suggestions, solve problems, and lend their own influence to your program.

I can't speak for the monkeys, but in most organizations this means that a lot of the default *behavers* have come to one of several conclusions:

"If he and she and the two from down the hall think this thing could work, maybe I should take another look at it. They're almost always right about this kind of thing."

"Wow! I didn't know this many people were behind this. It's going to be harder to ignore them than to help them."

"Yikes! I can't believe how much easier that looks. How did I get stuck doing it this old crummy way?"

"Nobody's thanked me for keeping up the old Forest Associates traditions in nearly a week. They all seem to be congratulating Mr. Maple, the guy who brought in all that business by trying the new approach. I'm beginning to think maybe they're on to something."

Critical mass is really about using the power of numbers to your advantage. The way to change behaviors in an organization is to gradually increase the number of behavers who share your point of view. Stop worrying about one person, or one manager, or one vice president, or one monkey, or the top monkey. Just keep building your critical mass, and the organization will follow.

I'm sure your next question is: "How do I get there?"

Let's start with a more precise definition of the challenge you face.

The first thing you should know is that despite appearances, defiant behavior is *not* your worst problem.

It's obvious that defiant behaviors will hurt your ability to adapt to the changing marketplace. No disagreement, there. The gap between the defiant behavers' attempts to protect the status quo and your need to re-align that status quo to better fit the constant change in the marketplace is extremely clear—maybe even too clear.

Their "extremism," if we can call it that, can distract you from the real challenge you face in reaching critical mass. Remember the numbers we discussed earlier?

Design: 20 percent

Default: 60 percent

Defiant: 20 percent

If we reduce this to a simple numbers game, where are you more likely to find the "recruits" you need to reach critical mass? Note that if you were to somehow miraculously convert all of the defiant behavers into design behavers you'd have only reached a standoff. (And, frankly, if I saw something that unlikely happen in my workplace, I'd be worried enough that I think I'd join the default group myself!)

No, just by the sheer weight of their numbers, the default group is the biggest obstacle you face in reaching critical mass. You will need to find enough converts from that camp to reach the 101st-monkey level.

Appearances would also seem to suggest that it should be easier to convert a default behaver into a design behaver than to drag a defiant one all the way across the spectrum of behavior. Again, appearance would be wrong!

In fact, default behavior can be extremely difficult to change, because it's much easier for default behavers to justify the way they act. For example: "I couldn't possibly be harming the organization. I'm just doing my job the way I have always done it. The way you taught me to do it. The way you pay me to do it. As soon as you tell me to do it differently, then I will go along. Just keeping my head down, doing my job . . . how could I be harming the organization?"

"At least I'm not over there throwing rocks and calling names and resisting change like those guys are."

In the meantime, what's happening to the default behaviors relative to your customers and your marketplace? Yes . . . the gap between them keeps getting bigger. The same developments and changes that led you to understand that your organization needed to change are now farther away. The market doesn't sit still.

I said this earlier, but I need to repeat it: If you are doing your job the same way you were two years ago, you are almost certainly out of alignment with your customers. It could be that if you are doing it the same way you did two months ago, you are out of alignment.

And the marketplace is moving away from the people with default behaviors just as surely and just as quickly as it's moving away from the people with defiant behaviors.

This can be a tough pill to swallow, because all of us at one point or another—even me, even you—have demonstrated default behavior. Every time you've gone to a workshop, a conference, a seminar, and every time you've listened to top management or a consultant talking about change in your organization, when your response has been along the lines of:

"How can I possibly be harming the organization—I'm just doing my job?"

"That sounds great but I don't see how it applies to me."

"I'll wait until they send a memo around spelling the whole thing out."

"I'll wait to see what the vice-presidents do and follow their lead."

"I'm not sticking my neck out on this one."

You've become part of the problem instead of part of the solution. There's an invaluable lesson in this kind of experience. You need to recognize why you adopted a default response in a given situation—it's going to make it a lot easier for you to understand and appreciate just how difficult change can be for some people, and why, in general, people resist change. (In other words, why 80 percent of the people in the chart we looked at earlier are not in the design category already.) But it should also make it crystal-clear where to find your candidates for recruiting into design behaviors.

RECRUITING DEFAULT INTO DESIGN

So what you need to do is to constantly be recruiting default behavers into design behavers. Get your critical mass by recruiting from that 60 percent of the workplace that's demonstrating default behaviors—and get them to grow into design.

As noted agent of change Willie Sutton famously said, "I rob banks because that's where the money is." *You'll* find your best targets among the ranks of the skeptical.

The opportunity here should be clear. So should your goals. Think about how much better off your organization would be if you could recruit all of the defiant behavers into default behavior, and at the same time, recruit some of the default behavers into design behavior. This is what the ideal change-adaptive organization looks like: 50 percent design and 50 percent default. (This is ideal and idealistic. In the real world you will never get this mix. Remember, we are talking about behaviors, and we all demonstrate all of the three types of behaviors). Think about how much faster your organization could implement changes that aligned you with your customers.

The 50 percent of design behavers will be in charge of tracking your customers and the marketplace: "Where'd they all go? Oh, there they are! We've got to get over there, pronto!"

In turn, they'll push the default behavers: "Come on, come on, come on. Look, they're over there, now. We've gotta go!"

The default behavers will stall and delay: "Hey, hold on a minute! Don't be so impatient! I haven't finished my coffee. Let's save this for Thursday's meeting, okay?"

But eventually, under pressure from the designers, they will move. The great thing about default behavers is that they are not unmovable the way the defiant group is. With enough urgency, enough explanation, and enough accountability they'll get on board and help you make the change work.

It is this critical mass that you need to keep your organization constantly moving toward opportunity and away from the danger it faces if it ignores its customers.

TRAPS FOR MANAGERS

Trap #1: *Lack of urgency.* Don't underestimate how urgent this can be. You've got to take on the recruiting conscientiously and aggressively. Why? Because if you're not recruiting the default behavers into your group of designers, then who will? Right! They're going to be recruited by the defiant behavers.

managing DOWN

HOW URGENT IS "URGENT"?

In terms of long-term results, encouraging design behaviors may be the most important thing you do each day. It's important enough to put it at the head of your to-do list. Add a heading about recruiting staff who are reluctant to change—and then specific notes on how to approach and involve the best candidates in your area.

Individuals demonstrating predominantly defiant behaviors have this critical mass concept down to a science. The "strength in numbers" concept is probably hardwired pretty deeply into the collective unconscious of the human race—starting as a defense against roaming packs of saber-toothed cats and ending as a defense against roaming packs of change-crazy people out to disrupt my job.

People who exhibit defiant behavior know that the more people they have around them doing their jobs the way they always have, actively resisting the initiatives for redesign and reorganization, the less likely that there will be any real change. You can imagine their recruiting pitch:

"Here, kid, let me tell you how things really work around here. I've seen vice presidents come, and I've seen vice presidents go. They've all had their own ideas for how things were gonna change! You'll get an inspiring speech, and an informational meeting, and if you're lucky a free lunch, but in the end we all come back to our desks and do things the way we've always done them. You know why? They don't push us because they know if they do, nothing will get done. And they'd rather have the work done than get the changes made."

Scary stuff! Remember, inertia is a powerful force! So is resistance to change. Your own recruiting approach is going to have to be just as compelling.

Trap #2: *But it's my job to make sure that everyone in the company is on board.* "My job is to get everybody to buy into the changes. To get cooperation and compliance from everyone."

Let me be as clear about this as I possibly can. That's not your job! Your job is big enough and hard enough without having to spend most of your time trying to rehabilitate the 20 percent of the workforce who have decided not to cooperate.

This isn't a nursery, or even an elementary school. As employees, it's really their job to decide to rehabilitate themselves. They're big kids now—and, besides, unlike school kids, they're getting paid for attendance!

But the problem is much more than how these people *should* act. Anyone who's been in the workplace for more than a few years knows that "should" has very little to do with much of what goes on.

The real problem is by indulging these defiant behaviors, you send a strong negative message to the rest of your staff. For example: Let's say you have two people reporting to you. One has predominantly design behavior and the other is predominantly defiant.

The designer is trying her best, experimenting with new things, enthusiastic, on-board, showing initiative, rocking the boat, focused on the customer, aligning with the marketplace, getting criticized at times, even yelled at, has knots in her stomach, can't sleep at nights, but wants to keep things moving forward.

The defiant one holds steadfast to the status quo, doing his job as he always has, with no real buy-in, no enthusiasm, fighting everything that management tries, doesn't invest one minute of extra time on the job, grunts and groans—and sleeps like a baby every night.

And you aren't sleeping so well yourself. You are spending big parts of every day trying to figure out ways to get the defiant one to get with the program, to see things your way. Almost every day you have to have a short meeting in your office to try to talk him through something that's gone wrong. Almost every morning you walk right by the designer so you can get to work on the defiant one.

Here's the problem. What message does that action send? It tells the designer that the defiant one is getting all of your time and attention.

Now, you can have a calm, quiet conversation with yourself, explaining how the defiant one just needs a little more time and that after a few more not-so-calm, not-so-quiet conversations with him, you think he'll come around to your way of thinking.

Which is great for you! But it's really just a way of deferring any significant action on your part. Try to look at the results, and at your focus and alignment in this situation, and you'll see that dragging things out with your defiant employee is actually a default behavior on your part.

In the meantime, the designer is working hard, talking to customers, aligning with the marketplace, rocking the boat for better change, taking her lumps, has knots in her stomach, can't sleep at night—and what else is she doing? Right—she is updating her resume!

Because as you can probably imagine she is saying to herself: "I'm going somewhere where my boss appreciates me. Someplace where they show their appreciation for a design employee who works hard, talks to customers, aligns with the marketplace, rocks the boat, takes her lumps, has knots in her stomach and can't sleep at night by encouraging her, answering her questions, showing the rest of the staff that her work matters, and recognizing how hard she's working to make change work in the organization."

Remember . . . it is always the good swimmers who jump ship first.

managing *DOWN*

DON'T OVERREACT

Just because someone is updating her resume doesn't mean that she's given up on the company. Your best employees—including those who are committed to the company and want to stay—are likely to be the best at keeping their credentials, their contacts, and their resumes up to date.

You have to start thinking in terms of risks and rewards. Most managers try to bring everyone in their organization along with the change by spending 80 percent of their time on 20 percent of their employees—the defiant 20 percent. Why? Because they are the most vocal, the angriest, and the most trouble. Because the squeaky wheel always gets the grease!

Somehow we imagine that if we can turn them, the rest of the change will be easy. If only . . .

What are we trying to do with those defiant behaviors? Change them and motivate them. Quiet them and keep them quiet. Get them on board. Get them going along. We try to encourage them, communicate with them, share our vision with them, and convince them to buy in. We try to lead and manage and discipline them.

That's a *major* investment of time and emotional energy. And what do we get for our efforts? Nothing. Zero. The Big Goose Egg. I'm telling you that in my experience with change in organizations, the bottom line on this type of effort is the total loss of everything you put into it.

All you'll get for your efforts is stress and frustration, your stomach tied in knots, and sleepless nights.

These are adults. They have to make up their minds about how they're going to act. In this case, they've made up their minds to be defiant. And, believe me, almost nothing you can say or do is going to change that.

So what *should* you do with these people? Just stop doing it. Stop trying to get them on board. Cut them off. Freeze them out. Stop bribing them with your time. Try to minimize their influence. Don't ask for their opinion. Don't spend time trying to convince them.

Let them know what you expect from them and that their meeting your expectations is a condition of their employment. Be clear about it. Make sure they're still informed about what the changes are and what role they'll be expected to play. Be exact about it.

But *don't* invite them to brainstorming sessions, planning meetings, or any activity where their defiance can make your job of encouraging designers and recruiting defaulters more difficult. And don't try to hide the hard facts of their situation—that you are out of time and out of patience, and they are getting in your way.

Do be civil and supportive. You would ideally like to move at least some of them into a default role, but you can't do it at the cost of productive work with your designer colleagues.

managing *DOWN*

MANAGING THE DEFIANT ONES

If you don't feel comfortable about cutting your losses this way, at least plan to try it for a limited time—maybe a week or so. You'll be surprised by how much more you get done and how much better you feel about the workplace in general. If this strategy doesn't work for you, figure out some way to limit the amount of time you spend with defiant individuals.

On the positive side, focus on both demonstrating and rewarding design behaviors. Whether you attend or lead a meeting about organizational change, make sure to participate, to get involved, to ask questions that clarify ambiguous points, to ask how it affects you and what you need to do differently. When you find fellow designers, recruit them into your planning sessions, have them reassigned to your group, make sure they get the best assignments and the organization-wide exposure that they deserve. Make them team leaders, project managers, recognize them at meetings, give them extra resources and extra flexibility.

Not only will you keep more good employees, but you are sending a powerful message to the rest of the company—especially the default performers. You know as well as I do that default behavers walk the halls of your organization trying to figure out how to get maximum rewards with minimal exposure. And the more they see designer behavior getting rewarded, the sooner they are going to drop their attitude of disengagement and go after the rewards.

Make it subtle, make it a soft sell, just make sure that everyone sees that you are catering to the designers in your organization. Do this for a few days and see how your default (and even defiant) employees respond: "Uh oh! Something's wrong here! I'm out of the loop!"

As I stated earlier, this is not personal. It's about behaviors. It's about encouraging the behaviors you need and discouraging the ones in your way. As soon as your employee starts demonstrating design behavior, he will be back in the loop.

"Hey, there! Welcome back! That's just what we needed!"

The only real problem with this kind of reward/reinforcement strategy is that ultimately all three groups get paid on payday. And getting paid while you're behaving in a default or defiant manner certainly reinforces the undesirable behaviors.

But you'll find that most people aren't motivated purely by money—they're also motivated by attention, recognition, interesting assignments, greater flexibility, and the approval of their colleagues. And you have a *lot* of influence over these aspects of their work experience. It's just another form of getting paid, but it's a powerful one. You can change the mix of behaviors in your organization by changing who and how you pay in terms of your time, your attention, your energy, your influence, and your focus.

managing DOWN

THE BEST REWARD

Don't forget to reward yourself—remember you, not the company, are responsible for your health and happiness. Make sure you do things that make you happy and keep you healthy—so that you can stay positive and enjoy your work.

Trap #3: *The success trap.* This one is especially tricky! Strangely enough, the worst thing that can happen to a manager is to *succeed* at converting defiant behavior because the cost is usually greater than you can afford. But that one hint of success makes you feel like you owe the effort to all those exhibiting defiant behavior.

For example: "But I finally reached one of them. It took me twenty-four months, but I finally got him on board and now he is one of our leading advocates of change." Do you see why this is a bad lesson to learn? One employee . . . twenty-four months. I hope he is a *really* hard-working guy!

In many ways the process we've just looked at is at the center of change management.

The challenge is to reach the point where change advocates outnumber (at least in influence) the change-phobic.

Only at that point do you have a fighting chance to make change stick, and all of your efforts should be aimed at improving your mix of design, default, and defiant behaviors.

The bad news is that this process can be difficult and time-consuming. Like every process that involves groups of people, you will occasionally find yourself taking one step forward and two steps back. The good news is that you have plenty of candidates to recruit into your efforts—nearly 80 percent of the organization.

SUMMING UP

- There are three keys to managing people with design, default, and defiant behaviors: demonstrate design behaviors, reward design behaviors, and reach a critical mass of workers with design behaviors.
- Your main opportunity comes in recruiting default behaviors into design behaviors.
- Trying to recruit employees who are primarily defiant may be a lost cause. They may "rehabilitate" themselves, but you've got more urgent work to do.

09

CONTROL THE CONTROLLABLES

When faced with the head-over-heels complexity of change, the human mind has an unhappy tendency to short-circuit—overwhelmed by the new information, increased workload, difficult decisions, divided loyalties, and its own natural resistance to change.

The human mind also tends to see what it wants to see, hear what it wants to hear, and do just what it wants to do. In the workplace, this can lead to pure denial, as in "I'll just do my job and everything will be okay"; or to defiant workers defending their resistance to change as somehow protecting the One True Corporate Culture.

So how does your responsibility for change play out in the workplace? How should you act? How do you decide what to do? How can you tell if you're focusing on the right things?

The best strategy I've seen for resolving this kind of uncertainty is called "Controlling the Controllables." In its simplest form, this means learning how to focus your time and energy on issues where you can make a difference and learning how *not* to waste your time and energy on problems you can't solve. You have no doubt seen or read many variations of this. The seeds of this concept for me came from Steven Covey's Circle of Influence.

It should be obvious that in your workplace there are some things that you *can* control and some things that you *can't*. The trick is being able to identify those things you can control and then to get busy controlling them. Get started by making a list of your concerns about the changes you've experienced—in your job, in your ability to do it, and in your future. What are some of your concerns? Let's look at some typical examples:

"I worry that we're spending so much time on changing the way we work, that there's not enough time to get the work done."

"Now that everything is changing, what's happened to my career path?"

"How am I going to get the training I need to keep up with the changes in my field?"

Do these sound familiar to you? Here are a few more that almost everyone faces:

"It seems like we're always cutting back. Will I have the resources I need to do my job?"

"How can I accomplish everything I'm being asked to do in the time I have?"

"Will I even have a job six months from now?"

These are all pretty legitimate concerns, right? I'm sure you have a few unique ones of your own, too. But for now, let's look at a few of the more common ones in order to get some perspective on how much of these issues you can really control.

RESOURCES

One of the biggest challenges faced by organizations going through change is that there never seem to be enough resources to go around. Whether it's tangible assets like desks, phones, computers, or offices; or budget issues like increased compensation for increased responsibility, training to meet new job requirements, or staffing to help with changing workloads—changes in resources always seem to lag behind the blistering pace of change.

As a result, many employees feel powerless. How can the changes they're being asked to make possibly work if they're starved of resources? What's in it for them? Many are so used to working with limited resources that they don't even bother asking.

But let's take a closer look at your control over your resources. Are they really out of your control? Or are there some aspects of this issue that you can control?

Ask yourself: "Is there anything about my resources that I *can* control?"

Here are a few suggestions:

You have a lot of control over your personal resources—your experience, your energy, your focus, your creativity, your talent and, to a lesser degree, your time.

You control how you use the resources that you already have: Either being stingy with them to make them last as long as possible, or making sure they're used efficiently and for maximum impact.

You control whether and how you try to get additional resources. Do you complain to your boss and demand more? Or do you analyze your needs carefully and make a powerful business case to the decision-maker in your organization?

Within practical limits you can change the way you do your job so that the resources you have are enough to get by on.

Sometimes there's really nothing you can do to get more resources.

In this case, all you control is your response to the problem: Are you going to be frustrated and defeatist? Or are you going to be resilient and creative in your response?

Do you see how you really have quite a bit of control over your resources? Sure, it's not as impressive as getting a personal assistant or a blank check from your accounting department, but these simple steps, at least, are in your hands, under your control. You are not powerless or without options!

What kind of resources does it make sense to look for in a changing situation? Again, here are a few suggestions:

Ask for as much training as possible on new systems or programs. Ask for access to trainers for follow-up questions, and for access to documentation, people with experience, etc.

Ask for temporary flexibility in your hours, workspace, responsibilities, etc., to help you get the most crucial work done while things change.

Ask for temp staff help to get through special events like moves or relocations, to deal with backlog when changing systems, to help people who are spending a lot of time in training get their jobs done.

managing UP

USE THE RIGHT TOOLS

Software project management tools, organizers, and to-do lists have made it possible to keep track of hundreds of projects at once. They allow you to categorize tasks by project, by priority, by urgency, etc. In most cases, though, they're not good for keeping track of the goals that drive your entire performance. Make sure to keep a separate sheet of personal targets like aligning with customer needs, moving through the stages of change, etc., so that they don't get forgotten under the piles of simple tasks that you're responsible for.

WORKLOAD

Next, let's look at your workload. Almost everybody is worried about this, especially in organizations going through a reorganization. Somehow changing from plan A to plan B always means doing job A *and* job B at the same time, right? I'm concerned about this, too—about how anyone gets anything done when they're trying to hold down two jobs at once.

Ask yourself: "Is there anything about my workload that I *can* control?" Here are a few suggestions:

You can learn to work smarter, not harder. You can spend some time each day organizing your work—and trying to develop ways to get it done faster and more efficiently.

You can find out whether you can delegate some of your work to others.

You can make sure to ask others for help when you run into problems or can't get your work done on time.

You can use technology to help you get more done in less time— e-mail, text messaging, instant messaging, etc.

You can tap other resources that help you work more efficiently— from organizational tools to frequent meetings with your supervisor about your priorities.

You can systematically eliminate distractions from your workplace. You can develop a consistent, energetic, and creative attitude toward your work—even if your direction keeps changing.

And maybe most importantly, you can figure out what it is that you need to stop doing, or what you can let go of.

Just as with resources, it looks like you actually do control quite a few aspects of your workload. Again, it's not as easy as hiring a full-time staff of professional assistants. But these are concrete steps you can take to improve your workload and stop being overwhelmed by it.

What can help you manage your workload in a changing situation? Again, here are a few suggestions:

The tools you need to work efficiently and effectively. This can include technology, office equipment, and office services like copiers and couriers.

The training you need to do the job. Your company should and should want to train you to make sure that you're able to be as productive as possible with new technology, systems, processes, business practices, etc.

The direction you need to be effective, including clear explanations of expectations, priorities, and new ways of doing things.

managing UP

WHEN TO SOUND THE ALARM

Multitasking means walking the fine line between being productive and being overwhelmed. If you lose your balance, the worst mistake you can make is pretending that you haven't. If your multitasking gets out of hand, find a way to simplify or put some work off or ask for help. Your boss will appreciate your willingness to take on work—and your sense of responsibility.

Keep in mind that this list includes items that may be difficult for some organizations to provide. Not every organization will be able to deliver the right tools for the job, the right training, or even have a clear idea of what it is they want to accomplish. Sometimes, in the midst of change, it's difficult to bring all of these factors into focus at once. In this case, which is all too common, your job is to do the best you can with what you've got. Change moves so quickly that you may "outrun" your resources, but you need to keep running!

managing *UP*

SO MUCH WORK, SO LITTLE TIME!

Managing your workload is a tricky issue because it's hard to complain without looking bad. Try to keep your goals realistic. If you feel you're not meeting expectations, have a conversation with your boss about what the company really expects. In many cases, you'll find that they don't really know what's realistic under the circumstances and are open to suggestions for keeping your workload under control. Just make sure to come with facts and suggestions—not complaints.

Finally, let's take a look at one of the most common and most important concerns.

JOB SECURITY

Where does an 800-pound gorilla sit? Wherever it wants, of course! Job security is the 800-pound gorilla of the workplace—everybody worries about it, no one wants to talk about it, and most people are convinced they can't do anything about it. In today's marketplace, almost every piece of news you read reinforces these concerns. There's no way to predict if your organization's efforts to change will work or not. If they don't, you could be out of a job.

All kinds of companies (maybe yours!) are looking to save money by outsourcing jobs to other locations. It's increasingly difficult to predict future demand in a changing marketplace, and most companies are keeping a tight leash on head count "just in case ..." Even companies that are doing well are cutting jobs to lower their costs.

If you feel you have no control over your job security, your concerns can create a powerful drag on your enthusiasm and energy for work.

Part of the problem is to keep this from becoming a self-fulfilling prophecy! Ask yourself: "Is there anything about my job security that I *can* control?" Well, let's look at a few examples:

You can control your own performance—making sure that you're a top performer who consistently exceeds the expectations of your supervisors and your organization. You can get advice from supervisors or mentors inside the company on how to best position yourself as an indispensable employee.

You can take advantage of the information you receive in reviews or evaluations to make sure that your behavior is in alignment with your organization's future goals and plans.

You can work on becoming the kind of employee that your organization can't afford to lose—by working hard to understand the company's goals, by applying your best efforts to making change work, and by helping others to get on with the process.

You can take your lack of security as a challenge, and by trying new things, learning new skills, and gaining more experience, become the kind of employee that no organization can do without.

You can prepare yourself emotionally, professionally, and financially for the nearly inevitable twists and turns of your career.

You can develop a perpetual job search strategy—in which you're always learning, always in contact with potential employers, always up to date in your field, always seeking out new opportunities—so that job loss isn't as threatening.

You can redefine the role of work and job security in your life—so that job loss seems like more of a transition than a tragedy.

You can control how this uncertainty affects you—whether it upsets or distracts you or challenges you to do what you can to address your concerns.

It is the harsh truth that today there is no such thing as tenure outside of the academic world, and there is no such thing as job security in the workplace—no matter where you work or how long you've held your job. On the other hand, as you can see from the list above, there *is* quite a bit you can do to increase your employment security *and* hopefully lessen your concerns. So is your job security under your control or not? Look for what your organization needs you to do, and make sure you're doing it. While that doesn't guarantee you a job, you will have as much job security as anyone does these days.

REALITY CHECK #1

Of course, not everyone is completely comfortable with this approach. You've got to be pretty resilient and self-reliant to accept that in today's workplace being in control has some clear limits. It's not hard to see why this bothers people! Everyone wants to feel needed and competent, especially when work takes so much of your time and energy, and the prospect of losing a job exposes you to feelings of loss, rejection, and worthlessness.

A lot of people feel that I'm overstating how much control you really have over your work situation; that a lot of the "controllable" aspects are rooted in willingness and ability to leave a job. For example, you might respond:

"I am not about to leave this organization now matter what happens. I like it here. I get paid pretty well. I like the people I work with. I like what I do. I don't want to move. I don't want to be looking for a job. So how can you say that this is within my control?"

It sounds like a pretty powerful argument: those are all good reasons to keep a job. But the fact is that these are statements of choice, of choices you've made. Let's look at them a little more closely:

Who decides whether you like your organization well enough to stay?

Who decides whether you're getting paid enough to stay?

Who decides whether liking your co-workers is a good enough reason to keep a job?

Who decides that finding a new job is too much trouble?

I think you get my point. These are all judgments that you have to make. A different person might evaluate any or all of these differently. But it's your life, and you're responsible for making all of these decisions. Who decides whether to get up in the morning and go to work? You do! Who decides whether to quit because someone asked you to clean the coffee pot? You do!

Now, this may not be a conscious decision that you have to think through every morning. But you do have the ultimate control over whether you stay in your job.

This applies to every aspect of your workplace. You choose to keep working for your organization. You choose to keep working for your boss. You choose to keep working despite the changes, despite your assignments, despite your co-workers' idiosyncrasies.

The "bottom line" is very simple: You choose to work, and your organization chooses to compensate you. Your other options may be a little harder to accept, but you still have the ultimate choice.

REALITY CHECK #2

Let's look at a second "reality check." Because of the side effects of change that we discussed earlier, you may have lost a level of trust in your organization. You may not believe that you will see reciprocity or a fair return for the time and energy that you've invested in your job or organization.

I hear statements like this quite a bit: "All of your advice sounds great, Karl. But I think you're ignoring one important fact. I've seen plenty of people who were great performers—flexible and adaptable and quick learners. And guess what? They don't work here any more. If you asked them, I don't think they'd feel that they had any control over their job security."

And there's some truth in that. Organizations make mistakes too. They don't always get the "bottom line" right. All kinds of things happen in organizations—for business or personal reasons or even due to plain bad luck—that don't seem to make sense. It can make it seem like job security, much less your ability to do anything about it, is an illusion.

But let's look at your situation a little more closely. Let's say that you've taken control of your job security:

You make sure that you have an accurate assessment of the quality of your performance.

You are always looking for ways to improve your performance and add value to the organization.

You make sure everything you do is focused on your customers.

You are flexible and adaptable and always trying to find better ways of doing things.

You have identified the skills you need to be both valuable to your organization and marketable to other organizations. (Fortunately, these are almost always the same skills!)

You have a plan for developing and sharing those skills with others.

You have a positive attitude toward your work, your colleagues, your organization, and toward change.

There are only two possible outcomes. First, you have turned yourself into an invaluable employee who will be kept on in even the "worst case scenario" for your organization. And that's because you are the most likely to adapt to and capitalize on the changes your organization will make to survive.

But let's look at the second outcome, your own personal "worst case scenario." Let's say that, for whatever reason, be it logical or illogical, deliberate or accidental, avoidable or inevitable, you lose your job. Think about the results of following my advice in this situation. Don't you think that the time and energy that you have invested in *yourself* will pay off? Don't you think that by controlling the things you can control in every aspect of your job, you have turned yourself into a top candidate for almost any job in any other organization, as well as, and maybe even more importantly, more capable of dealing with the difficulties of being unemployed?

managing *UP*

THE PRICE OF FLEXIBILITY

Being flexible should not mean getting stuck with the jobs nobody else wants. Make sure you keep a list of jobs you'd like to get involved with or learn about and share them with your boss regularly—maybe during annual reviews, if your company has them. Become a student of the industry versus a student of the job. Always be aware of future needs in your field and be equipping yourself to meet those needs.

You have made yourself employable And though "job security" in the New Business Reality is an illusion, employment security is not. And your employment security is 100% within your control.

THIS IS NOT A TRICK!

It may seem like my take on "Controlling the Controllables" is nothing more than an attempt to redefine the word "control" so that it simply means "influence" or "affect." Anyone can understand how they can "affect" their job security, right? I am trying, however, to get you to expand your understanding of where you can make a profound difference in both your life and your career.

This understanding is not only critical to deciding where you should spend your time and energy, but it is *more accurate* in terms of describing your influence in your organization. My goal is to make you see that you have more control over things than you think you do. I'm also suggesting that your opportunity to take control in your organization has never been better.

As we've seen, change in organizations creates ambiguity and uncertainty, and you're going to find that a lot of people in your organization are walking around doing nothing more productive than rolling their eyes, shrugging their shoulders, and shaking their heads. They have lost the certainty and clarity that they need to be productive at work, and they're going to be eager to find someone who can answer their question: "Well, what should we do?"

Your boss, your supervisors, upper management, and even the vice presidents are going to appreciate getting some straight answers from someone clearly invested in resolving the issues caused by change. The better your answers are, the more latitude you'll get to implement them. And *that* sounds like more control to me.

We all have a limited amount of time and energy. You have to determine where you invest yours. You can either invest it in the things that you can control or you can waste it working on and worrying about things that you can't control. If you stick with the ones you can control, you're going to get much better results.

In Control

I'm sure that you have co-workers who are always upbeat, positive, effective, not stressed, and not frustrated. They always seem to get more done, don't they? What's it like working with them? It's a positive experience, right? These are people who have learned to focus their time and energy on the things they can control! They seem more happy and relaxed than most of your colleagues because they *can* get things done, they can be effective, they feel competent. And they're not spending hours out of every day butting their heads against problems that they can't do anything about.

Out of Control

I'm sure you also have some co-workers who aren't so happy; who are stressed out, worried, frustrated, and ineffective. In most cases, it's because they have chosen battles they can't win, struggles with problems that they *don't* control! And if you find yourself going home at night feeling whipped and beat and frustrated, wondering why you can't seem to get anything done, chances are that you are investing too much in things you can't control.

What happens if you run up against a task or a problem that you really can't control? Remember that you do control how you let it affect you. Do you get rattled? Or do you get busy? Do you complain to your boss? Or do you try to talk to the person in your organization with the most experience with related problems? You control which of these two paths you'll take and therefore the results you're going to get.

One key to becoming an agent of change is to develop an accurate idea of who you are, what you're doing, what you're capable of, and what role your organization needs you to play as it struggles with change. Again, it's not necessary to find a perfect fit or to be perfect—very few people have that kind of control over themselves, or their situation!

Taking charge of your controllables isn't a cure-all—there are going to be tasks and situations where it doesn't work. But in my experience it is one of the most powerful and effective ideas that you can take from this book.

SUMMING UP

- Many people in organizations going through a difficult change feel powerless. They feel as if they've lost control of some of the most important aspects of their work.
- You can regain a sense of control if you start to focus on issues where you can make a difference and stop wasting time on those where you can't.
- People who feel that they've regained at least some control over their work are happier, more productive, more satisfied by their work, more fun to be around—and more employable!

CONCLUSION

WHAT ARE YOU GOING TO DO ABOUT IT?

I am a big believer in choice. Our society is based on freedom of choice. Our organizations are designed around the choices our customers make. Our careers are based on individual choices we make, based on our values and our abilities.

Yes, this is still a free country. You don't *have* to be a part of change. But you also need to be crystal clear on the consequences of your choices. The organization you work for is also free to do what it wants, or what it thinks is in its best interests. And if you decide that you're not interested in committing yourself to change, they have every right to say, "Well, you've made your choice. And now we're making ours," as they remove your name from the phone list, the mail drop, and the payroll.

You need to take personal responsibility for the process of change in your organization. This isn't the same as total control, but it is the same as total accountability.

This level of personal responsibility can be a little frightening. But the alternatives are even worse—working in organizations that can't compete, following rules that don't apply, disappointing your customers, your co-workers, and yourself.

Every time that you pick up your paycheck, you agree to that accountability. In the New Business Reality, this means not "just doing my job, ma'am" but doing your job plus whatever else is necessary to move your organization forward.

It can be a tough adjustment to make. It was easier when all you had to do was a simply defined, straightforward job that you knew and understood. But the expanded sense of responsibility required by the New Business Reality also means that it's your job to take risks, to try new things, to learn new things, to venture into unknown territory to find new ways to get the job done.

And if you are successful, it won't be because you hunkered down with the masses, memorized the manual, or followed the rules. It will because you went out and created the change that your organization needed.

"Agent of change" could be the best job description you'll ever have!

APPENDIX

15 KEYS TO SUCCESS IN THE NEW BUSINESS REALITY

The place where you work is now in a constant state of change. Competition comes from every corner of the globe. New technologies, innovative practices, and higher expectations have made long-term, stable relationships between businesses, employees, and their customers a thing of the past. "What have you done for me lately?" is more than a slogan—it's the way we do business today.

As a result, every organization—including yours—is on the brink of extinction, with your products, services, and your job only minutes from being obsolete. What you do is most likely being done better for less, just down the street, in another part of your building, or on the other side of the world.

The "old days," when companies acted more like the parents of a talented if unruly group of children, are gone forever. Today, most organizations can only afford to support those employees who care enough to give their very best—only those workers who care about the customers, and only those who care enough about the organization to take responsibility for its success—as well as their own.

Your choice is simple—whether to join the legions of employees who can't move beyond complaining about the frustrations and limitations of their job, who use the difficulties created by constant change as an excuse for not changing—or to decide that you're going to do something about it, making it your business to understand and benefit from these changes.

The good news is that your path to success is clear. The responsibility is now exactly where it should be: squarely on your shoulders. It's your responsibility to educate yourself, to make yourself marketable, to create your own employment security. You are responsible for your on-the-job performance, for your lunch, and for your future.

Success in this New Business Reality is based on knowledge: Who has it. Who can get it. Who can use it. Your success depends on your knowledge of your job, your organization, your industry, your profession, your customer's business and industry. But it depends especially on your understanding of what it takes to get the job done—the talents and experience that you need to create the value that your company's business depends on.

Today's organizations require a new set of skills—and it's your responsibility to identify and develop them. Let's take a quick look at what it takes to make it in the new world of work.

KEY #1

Set Higher Standards for Yourself

According to the management expert Peter Drucker, we are in the age of the knowledge worker. A "knowledge worker" is a new breed of employee who creates value by processing information to define and solve problems. Are you a knowledge worker? Don't you use, manipulate, enter, access, process, or create information? Aren't you expected to define and solve problems?

With the advent of global communications and competition, expectations are higher for every worker in every organization—regardless of what kind of business you're in. It's not good enough to simply "do the job" any more. Today you also are expected to contribute your ideas and intellect and to take responsibility and initiative for improving the way your organization works. At a minimum, you're expected to know your job, know your industry, track the developments in technology, methodology, and business practices that affect your employer, and evaluate how those changes affect your work. You also need to know your competition—understanding how they approach similar problems and opportunities and what kind of competitive challenges they present.

There are critical differences between knowledge workers and workers in previous eras that raise the bar for your performance. A knowledge worker's work is never done. There is no set number of widgets or billable hours that quantify success. Your work is only done when you have out-thought, out-innovated, and out-marketed your competition. This kind of competition rewards multiple approaches, frequent failure, and persistence. You need to develop your own benchmarks for success and make it your job to exceed them.

Every time you succeed, you raise the bar for your future performance. A great sales year is always followed by a higher revenue target. Your job is to come up with the next breakthrough, or program, or initiative, that will, inevitably, raise the bar again! There's no time to rest on your laurels. Success breeds new challenges. The competitive marketplace will always take your innovation and use it to ratchet up your competition. You need to anticipate this up-cycle; only if you continue to set the bar high do you stand a chance of getting ahead of your competitors.

Setting higher goals, standards, and expectations for yourself marks you as a person who is committed to your organization's success, as a top performer and a potential leader within the organization. As Peter Drucker put it, "Leadership is lifting a person's vision to higher sights, the raising of a person's performance to a higher standard." Start with yourself, and your influence within your organization will grow as a result.

Here are some suggestions for meeting today's higher expectations:

○ Look for ways to raise your standards and expectations for yourself. It's better to get ahead of changes in the workplace than to be forever trying to catch up.

○ Keep your eyes open for indications from your boss, your colleagues, or your customers that you need to raise your standards. Ask for clarification if you're not sure.

○ Volunteer to take on new tasks or to cross-train to get a broader understanding of your organization's business.

○ Keep up to date on developments in your company, your industry, and the technology, legislation, or markets that affect it.

KEY #2

Set a Fast Pace

New technologies and new developments in business operations will continue to increase the already rapid pace of change. In the past, organizations could actually plan to deal with change. Disruptive changes to their business came along at a much more manageable pace, and they had time to hold meetings, bring in consultants, and in general assimilate the change in an orderly way. Today, changes of all kinds and degrees appear much more frequently and unpredictably, giving organizations little time to prepare or recover.

Setting a faster pace means developing your personal ability to cope with the symptoms of rapid change: stress, frustration, and fatigue. Remember, this doesn't necessarily mean just accelerating what you're already doing. Sometimes it means making better decisions about your priorities. Sometimes it even means letting go of tasks that aren't as critical. In this stressed-out environment, knowing what not to do is almost as important as knowing how to do it.

In the future, the pace will only quicken. In the Old Business Reality, speed could kill. Decisions made without proper research, plans executed without proper planning, were recipes for disaster in that carefully planned, one-step-at-a-time era. In the New Business Reality, lack of speed can be just as deadly—crippling good products, organizations, and careers.

As we've seen, it's not enough to "just do your job." For every time you stop to "just do your job," you'll end up spending much more time catching up, and trying to put your competitive strategy back on track. The only practical response is to get better at handling change so that it doesn't stress you or your organization to the point of fatigue and inaction. This involves both a clear understanding of the personal "mechanics" of change and, as I've discussed, substantive alterations to the way both you and your organization deal with change on a daily basis. Your goal should be to develop a level of comfort with change that allows you to do your best work despite the rapid shifts in direction.

Here are a few suggestions to help you handle the faster pace of change:

○ Recognize that "slow and steady" no longer wins the race. In the New Business Reality, the race really does go to the swift.
○ Make taking action your highest priority whenever you can. If you absolutely need more research or an approval, get started on it immediately. Recreating lost opportunities is *not* a workable strategy.
○ Avoid breaking tasks into a sequence of consecutive steps. It may look neater on a plan, but it inevitably wastes time on your project.

○ Make decisions and move forward, even if you don't have all the facts. You'll make mistakes, but it's easier to fix mistakes than to find new opportunities.

○ Track and evaluate your results as quickly as possible. This means that you can start with a basic direction and turn it into an effective plan as you go.

KEY #3

Stay Positive

When someone begins to confuse negative thinking with critical thinking, it's a telltale sign that the person is having a hard time adjusting to change. The stresses and frustrations that go along with change make negative thinking easy. How much intelligence or imagination does it take to criticize a new idea that's not quite fully formed? How hard is it to skewer a new initiative that might really move the company forward but requires a difficult reorganization?

Whining and complaining about change doesn't contribute to, improve, or advance anything. It doesn't add value, provide solutions, or help you deal with the change. It certainly won't make you feel better about the hard work you're doing. And it's unfair to let your unhappiness undermine your colleagues' morale.

You need to be at your best if you're going to deal with change successfully. How can you possibly be as focused and flexible as you need to be while you're carrying around all that baggage?

Having a positive attitude, on the other hand, can make your work seem easier and more rewarding. How you get along with others, how you treat customers, and how well you work in a team go a long way toward determining just how effective and successful you are.

Every day is a new day. It gives you a fresh chance to perform. A new lease on your professional life. An opportunity to prove that you are committed to your organization and that you have something valuable to contribute. This doesn't mean that you have to like everyone or everything that comes up at work. Hardly anybody does! But you do need to keep a careful watch on your behavior, countenance, demeanor, and your tone of voice—especially when you hear yourself start to complain. Sharing your unhappiness with others is almost always counterproductive.

Here are a few suggestions for maintaining a positive attitude despite the challenges of change:

○ Try to stay engaged and involved in your work, especially the challenging parts. The more you can contribute, the faster these will seem more manageable and less stressful.

○ Every time you find a problem bothering you, try to switch your focus to developing a solution.

○ It's natural to complain a little. Everyone does it. But remember that it's part of a problem, not a solution, and try your best to keep it in check.

○ Try to bring a clean slate to every project or meeting. The less energy you're putting into events in the past, the more you can focus on solutions for current problems.

○ Remember that many times, it's not what you say, but how you say it. Putting a positive spin on something helps it go over more easily.

○ Give everyone else the benefit of the doubt. Or at least as much as you'd like them to give you!

KEY #4

Stay Confident

Maybe you're afraid to speak up. To disagree. To share your opinion. Afraid for your job. Afraid for your future. Afraid of your boss, and especially your boss's boss. Fear like this can be absolutely debilitating.

Fear can keep you from contributing your talent, your judgment, and your experience to your organization. It can drag you down into a vicious cycle. The natural reaction is to lay low, to hunker down, to stop contributing and stop taking risks. This may lower your stress level in the short run, but in the long run it not only hurts your organization, but it hurts you. If you're focused on avoiding risk instead of on doing your job, your work will suffer, which leads directly to more fear.

What exactly are people so afraid of? What someone will think of them? That someone might not like them if they speak up? That their ideas are stupid?

Even if all if these were true, which is unlikely, employers are looking for people willing to step up, speak up, share their ideas, and make a few mistakes in order to make a contribution. Organizations are starving for new ideas, ways to improve, to innovate, and are desperately looking for people with the courage to speak up——to overcome their fears and try to solve the organization's problems.

Paradoxically, the best way to avoid your biggest fear—your fear of losing your job—is by taking risks, by being willing to make mistakes. And the best way to lose your job is ... to lay low, to avoid taking risks, to not call attention to yourself.

Find a way to take a few chances, to speak up, to add value to your organization despite your fears, and you'll have every reason to be confident.

Here are a few suggestions to help you become more confident:

○ Watch the pros at work. Identify "top performers" in your organization and watch how they deal with their fears, with rejection, with mistakes, with failures. You'll notice that it happens more often than you might think and that the main difference is in how they handle it.

○ Remember the adage: "It doesn't matter how many times you're knocked down, as long as you keep getting up again." Persistence is key to success.

○ Fail early, fail often, learn to fail gracefully, and learn from your failures. Failure is often the quickest way to accelerate your learning curve.

○ Practice makes perfect. The more often you share and contribute, the less frequently you'll fail. You'll learn to anticipate problems in advance and prepare for them. Preparation is another key to self-confidence and success.

KEY #5

Be Honest

Truthfulness. Integrity. Candor. Frankness. Whatever you call it, honesty is not only the best policy, but it is a fundamental requirement for successful organizations in the New Business Reality.

Too many organizations act as though information should be protected and manipulated. And that employees need to be "protected" from the truth—about an organization's finances, operations, prospects. Unfortunately, that prevents crucial information from reaching the very audience that should be using it to further the organization's goals. Too many individuals also believe they should get all the information handed to them in a pleasing, agreeable, form.

The flip side of this is that too many individuals want to be protected from the truth. They believe that any information—and especially any feedback on their work performance—should be processed into polite, indirect, easy-to-digest statements.

But there's already so much confusion, uncertainty, misinformation, and missing information in a market environment that you can't afford any inside your organization.

This is true for information passing from every level to every level. From every person to every person. Whether it originates from inside or from outside the organization. Comprehensive and unwavering candor is necessary for both business and personal success.

Everyone in your organization should be able to handle the truth—as messy and complicated and unfortunate as it may be. We are all adults. We need to start acting that way. The first step is to communicate honestly. And stop trying to protect people from the truth. Stop tip-toeing around the real issues. Let's stop moderating our words for fear of hurting someone's feelings or making them angry. And most important, let's stop pretending that people can perform at their best without the information they need. Managers need to communicate their strategies to everyone—early, often, and as clearly as possible. Be frank about the harsh realities, dangers, and pitfalls of operating in the New Business Reality. Be just as honest with people about their performance—your message about what it is and what it *should be* needs to be crystal clear.

Employees need to stop shooting the messenger. Just because you don't like what you're hearing doesn't mean you don't need to hear it. Ask insightful questions. Seek out the information you need and challenge your leaders with a clear commitment to the customer.

Everyone needs to make an extra effort to make sure that they're sharing the unvarnished truth. Ask questions about anything you don't understand. If something is unclear, make sure to get it clarified. It is easier to ruffle a few feathers with questions and comments than it is to recover the time you can waste if you don't have the information that you need.

Here are a few suggestions for honesty in the workplace:

○ Commit yourself to sharing information equally. Resist the temptation to play favorites with what you know.

○ Be as honest as you can in every situation. Develop a reputation for straight talking and sharing information within your organization.

○ Share as much information as you can without regard to who's asking or what they might do with the information. If you have concerns, share those too.

○ Focus on issues, not personalities. Make sure that your message gets through clearly, regardless of your audience.

○ Be a seeker after truth. If you don't know what you need to know, find a way to find out. Ask for examples or clarification if you're not sure what someone means.

KEY #6

Be Decisive

You've probably heard the popular paradox: "Not to decide is to decide." It's a warning that gets to the heart of the business process and your role in it. Not making a decision has its own set of consequences—which can be even worse than if you'd made the wrong decision.

The saying first became popular in what are sometimes known as the "turbulent 1960s," but as you can imagine the message is even more urgent today. The speed and scope of business has increased exponentially since then, as has the rate of change. Breakthroughs in communication technology mean that you face a constant stream of new challenges and opportunities while trying not to be overwhelmed by a flood of new facts and figures.

Today, the only way an organization can stay competitive is by making more and faster decisions at all levels. No matter what your job title or where you work, you are paid to make decisions—every day, all the time, to the best of your ability. To use your intellect, experience, good judgment, and intuition to make good choices for your organization.

Don't defer, procrastinate, or avoid your responsibility. Remember, every delay comes with a cost—in lost opportunities, to your competitive advantage, to your success in the marketplace.

Do you need more information? Go get it. Do you need to discuss the possible results first? Pick up the phone. Need to consult with your team? Call them together. If you can't make the decision on your own, you can manage the decision-making process. Make it as quick AND efficient as you can. Estimate how long it will take you to get the required consults, approvals, etc. and schedule an end date for the process. Stick to it!

Making no decision—leaving it up to your boss, saying "It's not my job," is a decision in itself. Again, with its own consequences. Keep in mind that decision-making is a core competency in every organization. How do you think your boss will respond to any attempt to avoid it? And do you really want to let the other decision-makers in your organization make decisions that affect your work and your future—without your input?

Here are a few suggestions for becoming an expert decision maker:

○ Decision-making *is* your job. Take responsibility for it and make the best decision you can.
○ Decisions should never be made in a vacuum. Use your resources to help you make the right choice. Your research should be as targeted and efficient as possible. What's the best source of information about industry standards? For competitive terms? How has your organization dealt with similar issues in the past? Who knows the most about the issue?
○ Evaluate your research for relevance—don't just collect it.

○ Make sure to take your customers' needs into consideration. Talk to them.

○ Trust your instincts. Aside from your list of pros and cons, you have a wealth of informal knowledge about your job, your organization, and your industry. Put it to work!

○ Weigh your options and then make your decision. You might be wrong, but you've still made a responsible choice. And you can learn a lot from your mistakes.

KEY #7

Be Flexible

In the Old Business Reality it paid to specialize. Be a crackerjack financial analyst or a direct channel salesperson, and set your sights on the highest levels of the organization. If you were good enough, and stayed long enough, your future was secure.

The New Business Reality has turned this conventional wisdom on its head. Instead of specialization, flexibility has become one of the key qualifications for successful workers. The reason is simple. With the dramatically higher rate of change pushing and pulling the organization in different directions from quarter to quarter, employees who can cover a number of different jobs and bring a competency that allows them to navigate constant change have become invaluable.

Organizations can't possibly hire enough experienced staff to address the new opportunities they've found in the marketplace or to handle new products or services that their customers have asked them to deliver. And laying off or even retraining workers every time the organization's purpose or mission changed would be impossibly disruptive.

This means that employees who have a broad knowledge of the company's industry and business, with competence in many different areas, are at a premium.

As Charles Darwin, one of the all-time experts on survival in difficult circumstances, put it: "It is not the strongest of the species that survives, nor the most intelligent that survives. It is the one that is the most adaptable to change."

Darwin's changes, of course, happened over long periods of time. In your organization, the equivalent might be a few weeks. You can take for granted that the company's business will change that quickly. The question is whether you'll be able to change fast enough to keep up with it.

Here are a few suggestions for making yourself an invaluable and flexible employee:

○ Your ability to be flexible is essential. How adaptable are you? Are you willing to try new things? To add new skills? To learn to do something you've never done before?

○ Volunteer to fill in while people are out of town or on leave. Any familiarity with a different job makes you a better choice than a new hire or a temporary employee.

○ Get cross-trained in other areas wherever possible. Your goal is to gain a broad overview of your organization's business and develop experience and expertise that can be used in any part of the business.

○ Get to know people in other functional areas within your organization. Trade ideas. Ask them what skills they use the most often. Ask how they learned to do their job.

○ Keep learning—all day, every day. Whatever you can learn makes you a more valuable employee.

KEY #8

Raise Your Learning Curve

In the Old Business Reality you had a chance to master your job, your system, your process, or your discipline. You went to school, learned a set of skills, then found a job where you could practice them every day. And you practiced them until you mastered them. Then you were done learning. If you had the time and inclination, you could teach your skills to the new kids on the block.

In the New Business Reality mastering your job is no longer only about what you learn. It's also about how well and how quickly you learn and—sometimes—how quickly you can unlearn things.

The increased rate of change means that you face steeper (quicker) learning curves more often. Because change happens so much more often, you may find yourself on several learning curves at the same time, at the beginning of figuring out change A, midway through adjusting to change B, and almost comfortable with change C. (Change D is just around the corner. You'll find out about it at tomorrow's meeting!) As these changes pile up, one after the other, you have to learn how to accelerate your learning curve—just to keep up with your job!

In the New Business Reality, learning is all about speed. Response, cycle, and manufacturing times continue to shrink, and the same has happened to the time for learning. So learning today happens on the job and on the spot. There's no time for test runs or practice; you must learn as you go. New piece of equipment? Plug it in and get started. (Well, maybe check the manual to make sure you don't break it!) New process? Put it in place and go. New product, service, or offer? Get the information out to your customers, and refine it on the fly.

This new emphasis (insistence!) on efficient learning is not optional. Unfortunately, if you don't keep learning, somebody else will. (Usually, your competition.) The minute you stop, take a break, or pass on a learning opportunity, you have given away some of your competitive advantage.

You also need to accept that what you learn has a shorter shelf life. Standards, practices, formulas, and techniques—they all go out of date much faster than they used to. So nothing new that you learn today can be counted on to last. In fact, there may already be a new standard, approach, or requirement that makes what you just learned obsolete. But that doesn't mean that you can discount the value of learning. The potential risk of not learning is even higher!

Here are a few suggestions to help you learn more and faster:

○ Always keep your eyes open for opportunities to learn—both formally and informally. Learning things you didn't know you needed to know can give you unique insights into how your organization works and how to do your job better.

○ Learn as you go. Experience is the best teacher. (Although, admittedly, it can be kind of stressful!) You'll learn things that no teacher could have told you.

○ Get as much training as you can from your organization. If you don't feel it's enough, supplement it on your own time and at your own initiative.

○ Identify the people in your organization who know what you need to know. Don't be afraid to ask them questions or for help.

○ Learn from your failures. Don't be afraid to fail; everybody does it. If you're not failing or making mistakes, that means that you're not doing enough.

○ Teach others what you know. The best way to master a skill is to teach it to someone else. They'll often return the favor by teaching you something new that you need to know.

KEY #9

Learn to Multitask

When you're faced with the multiple interruptions and emergencies that make up a typical day at work, you probably think to yourself: Just let me focus! Give me a chance to concentrate on one thing!

But the opportunity to focus on a specific project until you're done is one of the rarest luxuries in contemporary business. And like so many other luxuries—first-class travel, unlimited expense accounts, and sales meetings in the Caribbean—it's really a thing of the past.

That's just not the way business works today. Challenges don't come when you expect them, customers don't complain when it's convenient, and your priorities change on a minute-to-minute basis. There's never a right time, or enough time, to devote yourself to a single task. All of your responsibilities need attention, and they all need attention at the same time.

This is the pulse and pace of business today. It's unrealistic to think that you can remove yourself from the mainstream, shut your door, and be left alone. You are part of the team. You are part of the grid. You are part of the always-on infrastructure of information sharing and decision-making that makes business work.

You are going to have to do more than one thing at a time. That's a given. Multitasking is a skill, and doing it well creates value. Being able to talk with customers while preparing for a meeting; raising one issue while solving another; taking an order, generating an invoice, and mailing documentation during the same conversation—all of these require multitasking skills that will make you more valuable to your organization. Multitasking does not necessarily mean that you'll lose your focus. It does mean that you'll have to focus for shorter and shorter periods of time, and that you'll have to make intelligent choices about where and how to allocate your time, energy and attention.

Here are a few suggestions to help you multitask:

○ Although multitasking may not come naturally, it can be accomplished through conscious choices and effort, as well as learning how to prioritize.

○ Add "one thing at a time" to your list of anachronistic sayings. Right after "hold your horses!"

○ Pay attention to how the most productive people in your organization get things done. How do they handle multitasking?

○ One of the most critical parts of multitasking is setting and refining your priorities, your list of "what happens next?" These can be set and reset on a daily or even hourly basis, depending on the urgency of your tasks. Make sure to get feedback from customers and team members about whether you're getting this right.

○ Create shorter blocks of time in your plan for the day. For example, don't give yourself an entire morning to solve a specific problem. Give yourself an hour. If you can't get it done that quickly, then you can always reorder your plans for the rest of the day. But tasks tend to fill the time allotted to them, and you'll find you almost always use the whole morning if that's what you've scheduled.

○ Stay on top of and be ruthless with your list of priorities. Anything that concerns a customer issue goes to the top of the list! Background research or "touching bases" go to the bottom, in most cases.

○ Use technology to help you stay organized. Good task management software is worth two cases of stick-on notes.

○ Accept the idea that you can't finish everything. Your job is to finish the right things! You also have to give up on being perfect. For most of us, it just takes too long.

KEY #10

Use the Latest Tools

One of the biggest drivers of change in today's world, and the reason why change is accelerating so rapidly, can be summed up in a single word: technology.

Jobs, organizations, entire industries have been radically changed by the introduction of modern technology. The way we work, the way we live, even the way we think have been transformed.

Avoiding new technology, especially communications technology, is no longer possible. Your customers, for example, will expect you to adopt technologies that work smoothly with their systems. If you don't adapt, your competition will.

To live and work in today's world, you must be able to operate in this new digital environment. Computers and communications technologies are your basic tools—as basic as a hammer to a carpenter or a net to a fisherman. You must be comfortable entering, accessing, manipulating, analyzing, and evaluating information created with and communicated through this complex combination of hardware, software, and communications technology.

Today's organizations assume that you have the necessary technological competencies: e-mail, messaging, databases, and office software. Remote access, scheduling, inventories, auctions, work assignments—more and more of the traditional workplace functions are being replaced by their electronic equivalents.

So how do you handle the crushing change brought on by technology? There are two common "technology traps," that organizations encounter, and both of them can be avoided with a little planning.

One basic mistake organizations make is trying to update their technology across the board—automating every process that can be automated. The truth is that some parts of your business will lend themselves to automation better than others. Look for functions that others have successfully automated, whether it's sales, inventory, shipping, planning, etc. Then look at the specific way your company implements that function. Deciding whether or not to automate should be based on whether the change will help you serve your customers better.

Another basic mistake is making more work for yourself. With communications technology, for example, e-mail is a given, and instant messaging can offer customers real benefits in some areas. But at this point, innovations in the field are running far ahead of applications. Make sure you understand *why* you're introducing a new technology, and make sure that it won't hurt your productivity.

Here are a few suggestions for using technology to your advantage:

○ Make technology work for you. Ask yourself, how can I use technology to help me do my job faster, better, and easier?

○ Get rid of obsolete and outdated technology. Don't let your customers get too far ahead of you. Make sure your systems are up to their standards.

○ Learn everything you can about technologies used in your industry. What's worked? What hasn't? This may take some extra research, but you don't want to be blindsided by a competitor with an established technology advantage.

○ Make sure you're well trained on any custom or proprietary technology your organization uses. These systems can give you a significant competitive advantage, and using them to their fullest justifies your organization's investment.

○ Learn about industry standards for data exchange, order transmittal, etc. Making sure you're in step with the standards in your field will help you reach the broadest range of customers, including the most demanding ones. Your customers will thank you!

○ Don't get too far ahead of the curve. Let others be the guinea pigs for immature systems and technologies. Your customers won't be impressed by your high tech efforts unless they get better service.

○ Give your employees the best communications you can justify, but make sure you're not giving them an opportunity to goof off, adding unnecessary work, or implementing a system that they'll never use.

KEY #11

Take Direction from Your Customers

Your customers are more educated, diverse, demanding, opinionated, individualistic, and discerning than ever. They have more choices, more information, and more special requirements than ever. And at the same time, they are less loyal and more impatient. In short, they are completely unrealistic!

Or are they? They just want what they want. They're making demands that someone will meet. They decide what they'll order and how much they'll pay for it. And so, they're determining what you should offer and how you should price it. Remember, they're the only reason you are in business or, more accurately, can stay in business. Their expectations apply to all industries, from manufacturing to healthcare to finance to insurance to telecommunications to organized religion and even to food service. The list is endless, and no one is exempt. Every single thing you do is, or should be, affected by the ever-changing demands of your customer.

Here are a few suggestions to help you understand your customers' needs:

○ Know who your customer is. Make sure everyone in your organization knows who he or she is. Get it touch. Make suggestions. Ask questions. Ask for feedback. Build an ongoing dialogue about your business.

○ Learn as much as you can about your customers' business and their customers. The more you know about them, the better you'll be able to anticipate their needs.

○ Learn as much as you can about your customers' internal organization. Know how they make decisions. Know what impresses them. Know how their budget works, and learn their buying process. The more you know, the more you can provide a unique service that fits their needs perfectly.

○ Know your industry inside out. Know who else your customers are talking to. Know what your competition is trying to sell them. Keep up on new developments so that you can provide answers to questions your customers haven't asked yet.

○ Given that most workers spend more time with their colleagues than with customers, it's not surprising that it's difficult to put your customers' needs ahead of your own. You need to demote your internal "customers" to second-class citizens—behind the needs of your real customer. Your organization will find a way to manage, but without the customer you'll have trouble staying in business.

○ Make customer satisfaction your principle measurement of success. How quickly/well did you meet their needs? What could you do better next time?

○ Redesign your processes with the customers in mind. What can you do to benefit them?

KEY #12

Make a Contribution

In the Old Business Reality, every organization had its share of people who were content to just show up. In the New Business Reality, organizations are *not* looking for people who can just fill a seat, a suit, or a job title. They're looking for people who can contribute—to growth, to change, to the bottom line. They're looking for people with ideas, suggestions, improvements, feedback, results, outcomes, intellect, and performance. Employees who can contribute to success, customer satisfaction, productivity, efficiency, speed, short-term and long-term success.

I can't emphasize this enough: In the New Business Reality, you get paid to contribute. Every day, in every way.

Laying low, keeping your options open, staying below the radar, not sticking your neck out, are no longer acceptable. Just "doing your job" is no longer good enough, regardless of your role, title, tenure, job description, or comfort level, and regardless of whether you are listened to, respected, acknowledged, or even thanked for your contribution. It is no longer acceptable to sit through a whole meeting and not say a word. It is no longer acceptable to attend a workshop, conference, or training and not participate. You cannot sit in the back of a meeting, fail to participate, and then grumble that they didn't answer your questions or address your concerns.

You are a capable, intelligent, resourceful adult who knows your job and does it well. You know what needs to be fixed. You know what can be done better or differently. You know where the cost savings are, where the opportunities are, how you can improve customer satisfaction. You have a notepad full of ideas and suggestions. Share them. Speak up! Contribute!

Got an opinion? Share it. Have a thought? Express it. Agree or disagree? Let everyone know. Find a better way? Put it on the table. Think you can do better? Just do it. Learn something new? Spread it around. Know something I don't? Enlighten me. That's what you're being paid for!

Here are a few suggestions to help you contribute:

○ Forget about "It's not my job," or "It's not my responsibility." It is your job, and your responsibility, to contribute.

○ Speak up. Worst case? You're wrong. But if you don't speak up, it doesn't matter if you're right.

○ Share what you know. If everyone shares their expertise and experience, everyone wins—you, your colleagues, your organization—and most importantly, your customers.

○ Trust your instincts. Sometimes you just know the answer before you can fully explain it.

○ Trust your judgment. No one knows your job better than you do.

KEY #13

Get Results

Success today is measured in one way and one way only—results. Your results are determined by one group, and one group only: your customers. Your organization succeeds or fails based on what your customers think of your results.

Good intentions aren't enough. Good intentions don't satisfy finicky, impatient, demanding customers. Trying hard isn't good enough. Customers don't care how hard you tried if they don't get what they want.

Ideas are great. Innovation is great. Suggestions for improvement are great. But by themselves they're not enough. Coming up with one great idea after another is not enough—unless you can turn your ideas into solutions, deliverable goods or services that offer solutions to your customers' problems. Execution is just as important as invention. You get credit for doing. You get credit for results!

Organizations today use fewer people to get more done. This is partly due to technology, partly to increased productivity. Across the board, problem solving has been pushed lower and lower into the ranks of the organization. The best decisions, innovations, and solutions come from those doing the job every day.

So being a small part of a big machine doesn't excuse you from delivering results. Not only are you expected to do your job, but you're also expected to figure out a better way of doing it. A safer, faster, less costly, more efficient way of delivering what the customer needs.

Here are a few suggestions for getting better results:

○ Find ways to get better information about your customers' needs and about what others in your industry are doing to solve similar problems. Both sources are invaluable starting points for new ideas.

○ Where does your job fit into the process of delivering results for your customer? What do you do that leads to new ideas? What do you do to help execute those ideas? Look for opportunities to contribute to your organization's results.

○ What can you do to turn new ideas and innovations into tangible results more often? More quickly?

○ There are two standards that every new initiative should meet: "Will it help our customers?" and, "Can we deliver it?" The second question is as important as the first and should be part of your planning process from the beginning.

KEY #14

Redefine Performance

In the Old Business Reality, performance was defined as productivity, which was measured by output, outcomes, or a full outbox (accompanied by an empty inbox). How many things you made, did, filed, moved, or assembled, or how many people you called or contacted, determined how productive you were. Sometimes, just looking busy was enough. It was bound to have some impact on the business, and you would be considered productive and a good performer.

Today's definition of performance is more demanding, more inclusive, and more complicated—and productivity is only one small part of how it's measured. How you do your job matters almost as much as what you do. The methods, tools, and approaches you choose count just as much as what you produce. Are you efficient? Do you try to improve the way you do things? Are you open to changing your approach if it becomes obsolete or inefficient? Or do you just keep doing what you've always been doing, the way you've always done it, even though it's no longer effective?

Performance is also measured by how well you work with others in a team environment. The days of the lone wolf retreating to his office, cube, or workstation to turn out brilliant work are over. Your workplace is just one part of the interconnected world we live in. Every job is connected to every other job in some way, at some point, somehow, or should be. Ideas coming from Research and Development have an impact on Marketing. The retailing programs developed in Sales affect the projections made by the Finance department. Work-flows created in the Tokyo office affect the schedules in the London office. The efficiency of the first shift determines production constraints on the second, and so on and so on.

To succeed in the New Business Reality, your organization needs to take advantage of the collective strength of everyone in the organization. To succeed in this highly collaborative environment, you need to develop strong communication, interpersonal, and leadership skills. Performance is no longer defined as just the contribution you make to your job. It's also defined as the contribution you make to the team, the organization, and the customer!

Here are a few suggestions to help you evaluate your performance during times of change:

○ Stop focusing on narrow measures of performance—like a clean desk, an empty inbox, or answered e-mail.
○ Develop ways to measure your performance that reflect your contribution to your organization's overall goals.
○ Recognize that your performance is based on your contributions to both team and individual goals.
○ Re-evaluate how you do your job. Does it fit your organization's current needs? Or did you choose it because you're comfortable with it or because it's easy to measure?

KEY #15

Redefine Success

When was the last time you got to sit back and enjoy a job well done? Finished, done, over, completed, mastered, perfected, wrapped up, or finalized. They all sound pretty good, don't they? But in today's world these words are at best anachronistic, at worst fantasies. In the New Business Reality, they have been replaced by fluid, agile, mobile, adaptive, nimble, and ever-changing.

In the Old Business Reality, success could be measured by that "job well done." We could tell whether a change we made had worked or not by the results. We could identify, measure, and reward our own contributions. Our personal and professional satisfaction was tied to a project's completion.

However, that sense of closure—that we've finished the job, that it's done and over, and we can give ourselves a pat on the back before we move on to the next big thing—no longer exists. For a lot of people, neither does the satisfaction they used to derive from that closure.

In the New Business Reality, the job is never "done." Rather it is fluid, evolving, and ever-changing. Our customers change, or the market changes, and our success is determined by our ability to change along with it.

But that doesn't mean you won't ever feel successful or fulfilled. Today, satisfaction is based on your ability and willingness to change. It comes from your mobility, agility, and adaptability. It comes from your skill at hitting a moving target, the market, rather than shooting fish in a barrel. It comes from knowing you can shift and change to adapt to any new challenge.

Organizations need to redefine success, too. Success today does not mean completing the plan without regard to changing customer demands. It's not driving the company to one place in the market only to see that everybody else has already moved on. Like it or not, organizational success cannot be measured in years, projects, systems, or objectives. Success today is measured by satisfied customers, marketplace alignment, and unmatched innovation.

Here are a few suggestions for redefining success:

○ Forget about being done. It'll probably never happen! But you'll still be able to enjoy the completion of steps, phases, rollouts, trials, etc., that are part of the ongoing process.

○ Take pride in how quickly you can adapt to changes in your focus or workload. In the end, it's what organizations value the most.

○ Keep a close watch on changes in your workplace and the customers you serve. Look at them as opportunities for new business, rather than as threats.

○ Reward effort throughout the entire process, not just on completion. After all, you may start out with one program in mind and have it turn into something entirely different.

INDEX

ABOUT THE AUTHOR

KARL G. SCHOEMER is president and founder of VisionQuest, a multidimensional training and consulting firm. Karl has helped managers, teams, and organizations develop the skills and beliefs necessary to manage the change process toward increased productivity.

Through his company he helps his clients cope with change and improve productivity by addressing their individual business needs and in the process teaches them skills and behaviors needed for long-term success. His diverse experience with a wide range of organizations and industries, and his personal experience with organizational change, gives him credibility with a variety of audiences—from senior executives to large employee groups.

He has worked with over a thousand different organizations in a hundred different industries on five continents in both the public and private sector. His clients include *Fortune* 500 companies, small start-ups, and government agencies.

Karl welcomes your comments and feedback. Visit him at his website at *www.VQSolutions.com.*